THE RAPTURE

THE CASE FOR A POST TRIBULATION RAPTURE IN THE END TIMES

THE RAPTURE

THE CASE FOR A POST TRIBULATION RAPTURE IN THE END TIMES

TIMOTHY LIANG

MA, UNIVERSITY OF CAMBRIDGE

THE RAPTURE

The Case for a Post Tribulation Rapture in the End Times

Copyright © 2023 Timothy Liang

Forward Digital Press

Paperback ISBN: 978-981-18-7713-1

Ebook ISBN: 978-981-18-7714-8

National Library Board, Singapore Cataloguing in Publication Data

Name(s): Liang, Timothy.

Title: The rapture : the case for a post tribulation rapture in the end times / Timothy Liang.

Description: [Singapore] : Forward Digital Press, 2023.

Identifier(s): ISBN 978-981-18-7713-1 (paperback) | ISBN 978-981-18-7714-8 (ebook)

Subject(s): LCSH: Rapture (Christian eschatology) | Tribulation (Christian eschatology) | Eschatology.

Classification: DDC 236.9--dc23

Dedication

This book is dedicated to the Lord Jesus, from whom
salvation has been given to the world. May the truth of
your coming be made known to the world and to
all Christians as a testimony to them,
just as you have told us. Amen!

I also dedicate this book to my dearest daughter
Charlotte, my wife Joey and to my parents,
Karen and Kevin, for their steadfast love
and devotion in Christ.

To Ray and Ginger Crocker, for your unwavering
love and dedication in Christ.

Contents

Preface

Jesus told his disciples that in this world they would face tribulation and suffer persecution for his name's sake. He said: "In the world ye shall have tribulation: but be of good cheer; I have overcome the world." (John 16:33 KJV). Yet, there is now a widespread teaching in America popularized by the Scofield Bible that before the Tribulation or the big trouble, Christ will come to rapture the church out of the world, leaving behind only unbelievers and the Jewish remnant of Israel to go through the Tribulation.

Unfortunately, this teaching has now been exported from America by missionaries all over the world with tragic consequences – it gives false hope to Christians that they will be spared from the coming Tribulation. The study of the end times or "eschatology" has now in effect become "escapology", the idea that the church will escape the big trouble when it comes.

The call to shift back to the truth and to scriptures is now more urgent than ever. This book argues the case for a post-tribulation rapture with a thorough examination from the scriptures and debunks the dispensational teaching of a pre-tribulation rapture from an eschatological standpoint. Why this matters is precisely because it affects the way the church should prepare for the future – should we put our hopes in a rapture that takes us out of tribulation, or should we get ready to suffer tribulation and persecution when the Antichrist comes in the future?

I invite you to consider this book with open hearts and minds so that, whichever view you take, you may be filled with the full measure of knowledge of the rapture and the Second Coming of our Lord Jesus. May the Lord bless you and keep you and give you peace. Amen!

TIMOTHY LIANG
MA, UNIVERSITY OF CAMBRIDGE

Chapter 1

Pre-Tribulation or Post-Tribulation Rapture: Why does it matter?

I should begin this book by stating that although the rapture question is one of the more widely debated questions among Christians within the church today, it should not be grounds for division within the church. Too many Christians have become much too divided over questions of Bible prophecy that neither serves them any purpose nor does the church any good – all Christians share the common hope of salvation in Jesus Christ and the promise of his Second Coming – and the immediate concerns of the church should be on repentance and living righteously for God and spreading the gospel of Jesus Christ through whom the promise of salvation has been given. Christians should not divide over matters of eschatology.

With that in mind, the aim of this book is to provide a comprehensive defense of the post-tribulation view based on scripture and to allow the Christian to have a more informed view on Bible prophecy – it should not be used to divide

Christians. Our attitude to Bible prophecy should be – "even if you take a different view, I still want to have fellowship with you." And I have found this approach to be most helpful when speaking to other Christians with a different view.

There are two predominant views of when the rapture would occur in the future.

The pre-tribulational view holds that Christ will return before the start of the Tribulation as described in the Book of Daniel (also known as Daniel's Seventieth Week) and rapture all Christians (i.e., the Church) out of the world into heaven before the start of the Tribulation or the "big trouble", leaving behind only unbelievers – unbelieving Gentiles and the Jewish remnant which God deals with during the 7 years of Tribulation. According to pre-tribulationists, those unbelievers who turn to God and to Christ during the Tribulation period are known as tribulation saints and will enter the Millennial Kingdom in their unglorified, earthly bodies at the end of the Tribulation, while raptured Christians return to earth with Jesus in their new glorified bodies and reign with him in the Millennial Kingdom.

It should also be clarified at the onset that pre-tribulationists view the Jewish remnant who are left behind for the Tribulation as comprising only of unbelieving Jews; Jews that have accepted Christ before the Tribulation will be raptured together with Gentile believers during the rapture according to them. In this regard, John F. Walvoord, the preeminent scholar on the pre-tribulation view, writes in his book *The Rapture Question* that "*Israelites by natural birth, upon receiving Christ as savior, become part of the body of Christ. By so much they are cut off from the particular promises and program of Israel and instead partake of the new program of God for the church on the same basis as Gentile believers.*" (Walvoord, p. 64) Therefore, John Walvoord thought that when Jews accepted Christ, they would form part of the "body of Christ" and no longer be part of "Israel". Believing Jews are therefore "cut off" from Israel and will be raptured together with all Christians before the Tribulation. Israel, in the end times context, only refers to the unbelieving Jewish remnant according to pre-tribulationists. If these unbelieving Jews turn to Christ during the Tribulation period, John Walvoord writes that they would partake in the program and promises that God made to Israel during the end times: "*when saved in this period, Israelites lose none of their national promises.*" (Walvoord, p. 64)

The post-tribulation view, by contrast, views that all Christians (both Jew and Gentile) will be raptured at the end of the Tribulation period – Christians are to go through the Tribulation and suffer persecution before Christ comes. During the rapture, the dead in Christ will rise first, and after that, those who remain on earth who are still alive and left will be caught up together with them in the clouds to meet the Lord in the air (1 Thessalonians 4:16-17). They will receive "imperishable" glorified bodies in that instant (1 Corinthians 15:51-52). Thereafter, all Christians will return to earth with the Lord Jesus to establish his kingdom and will reign with him in the Millennial Kingdom and rule over the nations of the earth (Zechariah 14:5, Revelation 2:26-27, Revelation 20:4)

There is also a third view that Christ is coming mid-tribulation (i.e., after the Tribulation and immediately before the Great Tribulation in the middle of the 7 years), but this view is neither supported by scripture nor held by any majority of Christians – it is a minority view that we would not consider in this book.

The Bible is clear – and most Christians agree – that there will be a rapture of all believers (the saints and the elect) when Christ returns. This has been dealt with by the Apostle Paul in 1 Thessalonians 4:13-18. The real question however, is when should we expect Christ to return and rapture all Christians to meet him in the air? Is Christ coming secretly to rapture all Christians before the Tribulation? Why this matters has enormous implications for the church and for all Christians in the future.

The Implications of a Pre-Tribulation View

If you believe in the pre-tribulation view of the rapture that Jesus would come and secretly rapture the church before the start of the Tribulation, there are four necessary implications that follow from this view.

The first major, and rather comforting implication is that all Christians would not have to go through the 7 years of Tribulation (and the Great Tribulation that begins in the middle of the 7 years of Tribulation c.f. Daniel 9:27) described in the Book of Revelation and in the Book of Daniel. Jesus describes the Great Tribulation in Matthew 24:21 as a time of *"great distress, unequaled from the beginning of the world until now – and never to be equaled again."* Since pre-tribulationists believe that Christians will be taken out of the world before the big trouble comes, they believe that Christians would be spared from this time of great distress.

The second implication, according to pre-tribulationists, is that since we do not know when the Tribulation would begin, it follows that Christ may come imminently or at any moment to rapture the church to heaven, and the rapture is the very next major event on the prophetic calendar. Christians are therefore to prepare for Christ's imminent return which may happen at any moment.

Third, if the church is raptured before the Tribulation, then it follows that Revelation 4-18 focuses entirely on God's dealings with the national of Israel (i.e., unbelieving Jews) and judgments on unbelievers – Christians have nothing to do with them. This largely follows the pre-tribulation dispensational teaching of scripture, which views the church as separate from Israel and the 7 years of Tribulation only concerning God's dealings with Israel and unbelieving Jews. The implication is that the study of Revelation then becomes purely academic for Christians in this present church-age since they will be raptured to heaven before the start of the Tribulation.

Fourth, if Jesus is coming secretly to rapture Christians before the start of the Tribulation, and then coming again to gather his elect or tribulation saints at the end of the Tribulation to establish the Millennial Kingdom, it follows that Jesus is coming not once but twice in the future. According to pre-tribulationists, the Second Coming is "secret" in the sense that Jesus comes and raptures the church to meet him in the air before the Tribulation (1 Thessalonians 4:17), while the third coming occurs after the Tribulation when Jesus comes to gather his elect (i.e., tribulation saints) and comes down together with all the saints to the Mount of Olives where sets himself as King over the whole earth (Matthew 24:31, Zechariah 14:4-9). Notice that pre-tribulationists do not see Matthew 24:31 as a rapture but rather a "gathering" of tribulation saints who go into the

Millennial Kingdom with the Messiah where he reigns. In other words, tribulation saints do not receive glorified bodies when they enter the Millennial Kingdom. John Walvoord explains in his book *The Rapture Question* that during the rapture, Christ returns to earth to take his disciples from earth to heaven. Walvoord writes that this is *"in absolute contrast to what takes place when Christ returns to establish His kingdom on earth. On that occasion, no one goes from earth to heaven."* (Walvoord, p. 71) Therefore, in his view, tribulation saints would not receive glorified bodies but will enter the Millennial Kingdom in their physical bodies to populate it.

The Implications of a Post-Tribulation View

On the other hand, if you believe in the post-tribulation view that Jesus would come to rapture the church only after the Tribulation, it follows that the church (i.e., the body of Christ), which includes believing Jews and Gentiles, will go through a period of great persecution in the future, and we will have to get ready for it. This means that the church must get ready for big trouble!

Second, it follows that Revelation 4-18 becomes entirely relevant for all Christians and provides a blueprint of the events that Christians should expect to go through during the Tribulation. Christians are given an overview of what will take place in the future to prepare them for persecution and endurance through trial.

Third, since Christ is only coming after the Tribulation to rapture all Christians, it follows that Christ is not coming imminently, and Christians are to instead watch for the signs of his Second Coming and not be caught by surprise when Jesus comes again.

Fourth, post-tribulationists see the rapture and the Second Coming as simultaneous events when Christ comes to rapture the saints and the elect and meet them in the air, descend to earth with all the saints and the elect and establish his Millennial Kingdom on earth.

Consequently, what view you take regarding when the rapture occurs and Christ's Second Coming affects the way you prepare for the future. If you believe the post-tribulation view that the church is to go through the big trouble, then much has to be done to prepare the church to be strong for persecution and to faithfully endure suffering in the future. The necessary question that you would ask is whether Christians today have the kind of faith required to endure trials and tribulations or even widespread persecution in the future.

However, if the pre-tribulation view is right, then the focus shifts from preparing the church for the Tribulation to getting ready for the rapture – which is the next major event on the prophetic calendar according to the pre-tribulationists. If you pause to think about it, this has profound implications for Christians because, if you believe that Christ is coming imminently and at any moment, then Christians should get ready not for the Tribulation but for Christ's immediate return and live their lives in expectancy of his immediate return.

Admittedly, the pre-tribulation rapture view is also very comforting because it gives Christians a sense of hope and security that they would be raptured to heaven before the Tribulation comes – Christians would not have to endure the big trouble. They look to Christ's coming to rapture them out to heaven before the Tribulation begins. It is also a frightening thought for Israel and unbelievers as it would mean they would be "left behind" to endure the Great Tribulation.

Now the real question is not whether you believe in a pre-tribulation or post-tribulation rapture – the real question we should be asking is which view is the right one and supported by scripture. The reason why this matters is precisely because it affects the way Christians should prepare for the future – do we put our hopes in a rapture that will save us from the fiery trial? Or do we get ready for persecution and the big trouble?

There is a concerning shift in modern times from the early church's post-tribulation view of the rapture to a pre-tribulation view that the church would be completely removed from the Tribulation. This shift, as I will show in the next chapter, started in the late 1820s within the Brethren movement and was propagated by a man named John Nelson Darby who popularized the idea that the church and Israel were separate from one another and God deals with both of them in separate "dispensations", or time periods. John Nelson Darby subsequently went to America and shared the idea with two prominent theologians – C. I. Scofield and L. S. Chafer, both of whom helped to popularize the pre-tribulation view in America in the 1900s.

Tragically, this dispensational view of the rapture (i.e., the view that God deals with the church and Israel separately during the end times and that the church and Israel are distinctly separate entities) is now the predominant view in North America has been exported from America to other countries by missionaries all around the world. As we will see in the later chapters, this has profound implications for the wider church and especially for churches that are experiencing persecution, notably in China and Africa. It does little to nothing to prepare Christians to be strong for the local tribulation that they are experiencing daily.

Theologically, it has in effect caused the study of eschatology to become what is more widely known as "escapology" – the view that the church will escape the big trouble and God deals with the unbelieving Jewish remnant of Israel during the Tribulation period.

As David Pawson rightly notes, this pre-tribulation view is not based on any clear Bible verse that Jesus is coming to rapture the church out from the Tribulation, but rather from inferences and human logic that are not quite supported by scripture, one such inference being need for human beings to populate the Millennial Kingdom in their natural bodies in order to fulfill scripture. We will come to that in the later chapters.

To fully understand how the pre-tribulation view came about and its dispensational roots, it is necessary to trace its historical origins back to the Brethren movement in 1826.

Chapter 2

The Historical Roots of the Pre-Tribulation Doctrine

There has been much speculation and debate about the origins of the dispensational pre-tribulation rapture view. Much of the origins of the pre-tribulation rapture view can be traced back to the Brethren movement as far back as 1826 to John Nelson Darby, who was one of the early proponents of the Brethren movement in Ireland.

Brethren writer, Roy A Huebner, notes in *John Nelson Darby: Precious Truths Revived and Defended, Volume One* that Darby developed his dispensational understanding of the pre-tribulation rapture during a convalesce from an injury. Huebner records that Darby wrote: *"I saw that the Christian, having his place in Christ in heaven, has nothing to wait for, save the coming of the Saviour, in order to be set, in fact, in the glory which is already his portion 'in Christ'."* (Huebner, p. 17)

Darby learned that he ought to daily expect the Lord. In context, he meant that there were no intervening events that had to take place before the Lord would come for his own. Apparently, this view was due to Darby's understanding of Isaiah 32 when he *"saw an evidence change of dispensation in that chapter, when the Spirit would be poured out on the Jewish nation, and a king reign in righteousness."* (Huebner, p. 12) By this, Darby meant that *"there were no intervening events that had to take place before the Lord would come for His own. [The Christians] That was the heavenly side, for Isaiah 32 brought before him the earthly side of things [concerning only the nation of Israel]."* (Huebner, p. 12)

In other words, Darby thought that since his place was with Christ, and he saw the church as composed of only those who were united with Christ, then the one who had his place in Christ in heaven has nothing to wait for but Christ. However, since God still had to fulfill the promises He made to Israel in the Old Testament, Darby reasoned that Christ would come for his church first, and then followed by a change in dispensation where Christ deals with the future remnant of Israel in the time of Tribulation or Jacob's trouble.

It should be noted that not all in the Brethren movement shared Darby's view. Edward Irving, for instance, saw himself *"in an era of prophecy being fulfilled and that there were intermediate events that needed to take place before Christ would come."* (Huebner, p. 12) In *Christianity and Rabbinic Judaism: A History of Conflict between Christianity and Rabbinic Judaism*, Jonas Alexis records that George Muller, also one of the early founders of the Plymouth Brethren movement, had this to say about Darby: *"I am a constant reader of the Bible, and I soon found that what I was taught to believe [by Darby] did not always agree with what my Bible said. I came to see that I must either part company with John Darby, or my precious Bible, and I chose to cling to my Bible and part from Mr Darby."* (Alexis, p. 200) Darby's view, however, prevailed among those in the Brethren movement.

Charles H. Spurgeon, one of the most prominent and respected Bible teachers in the nineteenth century, held many irreconcilable theological differences with Darby. He was highly critical of Darby's dispensational views, and declared: *"Mr Darby is, to all intents and purposes, a thorough Pope, though under a Protestant name. He will never admit that he is in error; and therefore very naturally declines to argue with those who controvert the soundness of his views."* (Alexis, p. 199) In fact, Spurgeon had much to say about dispensationalists and was highly critical of their views. In his book *The Sword and the Trowel*, Spurgeon wrote: *"And first of all, do not, we beseech you, be cajoled by any appeal to "God's dispensational arrangements," knowing that, however various they may have been, his covenant has endured the same through them all."* (Spurgeon, p. 345-350) He continues that a difference in dispensation does not involve a difference of covenant. Spurgeon writes: *"It is a mere truism that Abel was not circumcised, that Noah did not observe the Passover, and Abraham was not baptized."* Spurgeon then rightly observes that it is impossible to say when one dispensation began and closed; it serves no practical use and only creates unproductive debates. He writes: *"Would you tell us when the Abrahamic dispensation began and when it closed? We had rather you did not attempt to guess for fear of a fresh strife."* (Spurgeon, p. 345-350)

Concerning the pre-tribulation rapture, Spurgeon was equally critical. In his 22 December 1867 sermon on *"The Great Mystery of Godliness"*, Spurgeon declared that *"They [dispensationalists] plume themselves upon an expected secret rapture, and I do not know what vain imaginings besides."* Spurgeon was deeply critical of systematic dispensationalism, preaching that Christians derived essentially no benefit from it and it was a distraction from the message of salvation in Christ. He declared that those who propagated such views were "sectarian" and more devoted to their "system" of theology rather than preaching Christ. Having said that, Spurgeon did not say much about the post-tribulation rapture either; he generally held a distaste for Bible prophecy and thought that modern prophetical works was a sheer waste of time and a distraction from practical work for Jesus. But it is notable that Spurgeon never saw eye to eye with Darby and was highly critical of dispensational theology and the way it divided the gospel into different time periods.

David Pawson, in his 1995 sermon *"Revelation Riddle: Will Christians Escape by Secret Rapture"* notes that Darby at some point went to America and shared his dispensational views with an American lawyer named C. I. Scofield and theologian L. S. Chafer. Scofield later wrote the Scofield reference Bible and incorporated Darby's pre-tribulation rapture views into them, while L. S. Chafer went on to found the Dallas Theological Seminary and remained its president until his death in 1952. Both of them helped to popularized the pre-tribulation view which is now the prevalent view in America among evangelicals today.

Michael Williams in his analysis on dispensationalism in *This World is not My Home, The Origins and Development of Dispensationalism (2003)*, writes that the "*Darbyist metaphysical distinction between Israel and the church is the sine qua non of classical dispensation theology.*" (Williams, p. 90) In other words, the distinction between Israel and the church is the basis of dispensational theology, and Darby saw this distinction as crucial to his dispensational theory that during the end times, the church would be raptured to heaven to be with Christ before God deals with the remaining Jewish remnant of Israel.

Due to the work of Scofield and in particular the influences of the Scofield Reference Bible, the result is now a widespread teaching in America that before the big trouble Christ would come to rapture the church and take all Christians out of the world before the start of the Tribulation. David Pawson points out that the Dallas Seminary in Texas which L. S. Chafer was its first president, and subsequently helmed by John F. Walvoord, now holds the pre-tribulation rapture to be gospel truth and its students have been taught this view ever since.

Further popularization of the pre-tribulation view came from American authors including Hal Lindsey, who in his popular 1970 book *The Late Great Planet Earth*, advocated a pre-tribulation rapture of the church. John F. Walvoord, the late president of the Dallas Theological Seminary also popularized this view in his seminal work in the 1957 book *The Rapture Question*, which we will use as the basis for discussion on the pre-tribulation view in this book.

I would just pause here to note one interesting observation that Darby never actually relied on the classic passages from the

Bible that modern pre-tribulational scholars like to quote to support a pre-tribulation rapture, such as 1 Thessalonians 4 and 1 Thessalonians 1:10. Rather, Darby based his understanding of the pre-tribulation rapture on Isaiah 32 and Matthew 24 that there was a different dispensation coming, and that Israel and the church were distinct. It was his view that since the church was already united with Christ, the church would not have to go through tribulation and there would be no intervening events that had to take place before the rapture.

In other words, Darby thought that Matthew 24 referred only to the Jewish remnant. He saw a Jewish remnant in the times of Jacob's trouble and understood that there would be a personal Antichrist over the apostate Jews. He reasoned that the church would not have to go through the Tribulation as judgment was only reserved for Gentile unbelievers and for the remnant of unbelieving Jews that had not yet been united with Christ.

It is noteworthy that B. W. Newton, one of the early founders of the Plymouth Brethren movement and a friend of John Darby, became increasingly critical of Darby's view that Matthew 24 only relates primarily to the Jews. Unlike Darby, Newton believed that the church was now comprised of both Jews and Gentiles, who have been made one in Christ. When Newton pressed Darby for an explanation for his dispensational views especially on interpreting Matthew 24, Newton recounted that Darby gave him the "Jewish interpretation" – in other words, *"the Gospel of Matthew was not teaching Church-Truth but Kingdom-Truth – and so on."* (Huebner, p. 84) Newton told Darby that if he admitted that distinction, he had basically given up on Christianity. In Newton's view, the "secret rapture" was bad enough, but this distinction between Israel and the church was worse because it implied distinct and separate ways to salvation for both Jew and Gentile.

It is interesting to note that before John Nelson Darby, there is not a single trace of the pre-tribulation view that we can find from a historical perspective. There is no evidence that the early church ever held the pre-tribulation view – and Darby's dispensational invention that Israel or "the Jews" represented God's "earthly people", while "the Church" represented God's "heavenly people", is a comparatively modern view that was never adopted by the early church. As we examine the scriptures on what Jesus and the Apostle Paul said on Jewish and Gentile believers in the later chapters, we come to the common themes of Christian unity between the church and Israel in Christ and the role of the church in Israel's salvation during the end times, which are entirely contrary to Darby's dispensational views.

Chapter 3

Shifting back to Scripture: Arguments Supporting a Post-Tribulation Rapture

#1 The plain and literal interpretation of the Olivet
Discourse in all three synoptic gospels
supports a post-tribulation rapture

The Olivet Discourse in all three synoptic gospels – Matthew 24, Mark 13 and Luke 21 are the clearest authority that we have concerning the timing of the rapture and the events that must take place prior to the Lord's Second Coming. In these chapters, the Lord Jesus himself sets out, in chronological order, the events that must take place on earth during the Tribulation before he comes. It is useful to set out all the events that must take place as seen in all three synoptic gospels verse by verse to get a clear picture of the timing of his Second Coming and the rapture of the saints.

One important point to consider here is that, since pre-tribulationists hold that Christians would be raptured to heaven before the Tribulation, Matthew 24, Mark 13 and Luke 21 are therefore addressed to tribulation saints (i.e., unbelieving Jews and Gentiles who turn to Christ during the Tribulation period). As we will soon see from a careful examination of scripture in all three synoptic gospels, it is highly improbable that these words from our Lord Jesus in the Olivet Discourse were addressed only to tribulation saints.

1. Before the Tribulation, many will claim that they are the Messiah, deceiving many. Jesus tells Christians not to be deceived.

Even before the start of the Tribulation, the Lord Jesus warns his disciples not to be deceived. He says, "*Watch out that no one deceives you. For many will come in my name, claiming, "I am the Messiah," and will deceive many.*" (Matthew 24:4-5) In the Gospel of Luke, it is recorded that Jesus said: "*Watch out that you are not deceived. For many will come in my name, claiming, 'I am he,' and, 'The time is near'. Do not follow them.*" (Luke 21:8) The fact that many people will come and say 'the time is near' before the start of the Tribulation sounds similar to what the pre-tribulationists are claiming, that Jesus will be coming imminently or at any moment now.

Notice that in all three synoptic gospels, the Lord Jesus warns Christians **before** the start of the Tribulation not to be deceived by false messiahs or false claims that He has come. These verses are at the very beginning of the Olivet Discourse, which signals Jesus' clear intention to warn against deceptions of his coming **even before** the Tribulation begins. The positioning of his warnings against deception – before and during the Tribulation – are quite telling that Jesus has not come yet. One has to wonder if the Lord Jesus was truly addressing tribulation saints in these verses – or if he is addressing all Christians.

2. Christians will hear of wars and rumors of wars – these things must happen first, but the end is still to come.

Next, after his warning against deception, the Lord Jesus says that *"You will hear of wars and rumors of wars, but see to it that you are not alarmed. Such things must happen, but the end is still yet to come."* (Matthew 24:6) The scriptures are clear that wars and rumors of wars must happen first, but the end is still to come.

3. Nation will rise against nation. There will be famines and earthquakes.

Immediately after hearing wars and rumors of wars, Jesus tells us that nation will rise against nation, and there will be famines and earthquakes in the world. He says *"Nation will rise against nation, and kingdom against kingdom. There will be famines and earthquakes in various places. All these are the beginnings of birth pains."* (Matthew 24:7-8)

It should be noted that the world has gone through a period of comparatively recent wars – including two World Wars in 1914 and 1939 – involving many nations and millions of deaths. Famines followed in the wake of World War

II with one famine costing the lives of 100,000 people in Tokyo in 1945 and the Soviet famine of 1946-47. The 2004 Indian Ocean tsunami caused by an underwater earthquake was among the deadliest of natural disasters ever recorded, with at least 230,000 people killed in 14 countries. Will there be more wars, famines and earthquakes? Probably, but we don't know for sure. Jesus tells us that these are just the beginning of birth pains.

4. During the Tribulation, Christians will be universally persecuted by all nations.

During the Tribulation period, Christians will be universally persecuted and hated by "all nations". Jesus tells his disciples: *"Then you will be handed over to be persecuted and put to death, and you will be hated by all nations because of me."* (Matthew 24:9)

Jesus tells us that there will come a time when Christians will be persecuted by all nations. It is interesting to note that both Mark and Luke mention the word "synagogues" which imply that that these verses were directed specifically at Jewish Christians – see Mark 13:9 and Luke 21:12-13. Matthew 24:9 does not however contain any reference to the word "synagogue" but makes a general statement of Christian persecution.

5. Many Christians will turn away from the faith and betray one another.

At the end times, Christians will be universally hated and betrayed even by their own immediate family members. Matthew tells us that many Christians will turn away from the faith – which implies that the Christians (Jewish or Gentile) are still around during the Tribulation. Jesus says: "*At that time many will turn away from the faith, and will betray and hate each other, and many false prophets will appear and deceive many people.*" (Matthew 24:10-11) This raises the question that if all Christians have been raptured out of the world before the Tribulation, then who are those people that will turn away from the faith? Is the Lord Jesus really referring to tribulation saints who have come to the faith during the Tribulation and subsequently abandoned the faith, as the pre-tribulationists would have it?

6. The world will become wicked. But the one who endures to the end will be saved.

Because of the universal persecution of Christians, the world will become wicked. Jesus says: "*Because of the increase of wickedness, the love of most will grow cold, but the one who stands firm to the end will be saved.*" (Matthew 24:12-13) In the gospel of Mark, Jesus is recorded as saying: "*Everyone will hate you because of me, but the one who stands firm to the end will be saved.*" (Mark 13:13)

The single commonality is that the Lord Jesus tells Christians to stand firm to the very end: "*the one who stands firm **to the end** will be saved.*" (*emphasis added*) The plain and literal interpretation of the words "to the end" implies that Christians are to brave through the Tribulation to the very end – they are not to be taken out of the Tribulation – otherwise how would Christians stand firm to the end? It seems quite improbable that Jesus was only referring to tribulation saints when he said this.

7. The result of increased persecution is that the gospel will be preached to all nations!

The amazing consequence of increased persecution of the church is that the gospel will be preached to all nations! Jesus says: "*And this gospel of the kingdom will be preached in the whole world as a testimony to all nations, and then the end will come.*" (Matthew 24:14) The Lord Jesus gave the responsibility of preaching the gospel to all His disciples – the Christians – who became missionaries around the world for the sake of the gospel. If the pre-tribulation view is right and the church is raptured before the Tribulation, who will be preaching the gospel to all nations?

8. The Antichrist appears in the holy place.

The Lord Jesus tells us that the Antichrist will set up the 'abomination that causes desolation' in the holy place and set himself up as a God. Jesus says: "*So when you see standing in the holy place 'the abomination that causes desolation,' spoken of through the prophet Daniel – let the reader understand – then let those who are in Judea flee to the mountains.*" (Matthew 24:15)

The 'abomination that causes desolation' is set up by the Antichrist or the man of lawlessness, who according to the Apostle Paul, "*will oppose and will exalt himself over everything that is called God or is worshipped, so that he sets himself up in God's temple, proclaiming himself to be God.*" (2 Thessalonians 2:4)

9. The Great Tribulation begins when the Antichrist sets himself up in the holy place (cf. Daniel 9:27 and 2

Thessalonians 2:4). Jesus tells those living in Judea to flee for their lives.

Jesus tells the Jews living in Judea at the time of the Great Tribulation to flee immediately: *"Let no one on the housetop go down to take anything out of the house. Let no one in the field go back to get their cloak. How dreadful it would be in those days for pregnant women and nursing mothers! Pray that your flight will not take place in winter of the Sabbath."* (Matthew 24:17-20) The sense of urgency that is stressed in these verses highlights the impending desolation of Jerusalem. In the Gospel of Luke, we are told that *"Jerusalem will be trampled on by the Gentiles until the times of the Gentiles are fulfilled."* (Luke 21:23-24)

It is noteworthy that these verses specifically concern Jews living in Judea. He tells them to flee from the area quickly – and to pray that their "flight" or their escape would not take place during the winter or on the Sabbath, where there is no available transportation. The urgency is expressed in the words *"let no one in the field go back to get their cloak"* – which literally means to drop everything you are doing and flee.

10. There will be great distress in the world and in Jerusalem.

The distress in the Great Tribulation will be a global event – all Christians will see it. Jesus says: *"For then there will be great distress, unequaled from the beginning of the world until now – and never to be equaled again."* (Matthew 24:21)

It is interesting to note that both Matthew and Mark mentions *"great distress, unequaled from the beginning of the world"* which implies big trouble that affects the entire world. This distress is so great that it will never be equaled in the world again. Luke, however, takes a more localized approach *"there will be great distress in the land and wrath against this people."* (Luke 21:23), implying that great distress will also occur in Israel and in Judea.

In other words, this great distress affects the whole world as it affects Jerusalem.

11. No one would survive the Great Tribulation had it not been cut short.

Christians would not survive the Great Tribulation unless it had been cut short for the "sake of the elect". Jesus says to his disciples, *"If those days had not been cut short, no one would survive, but for the sake of the elect those days will be shortened."* (Matthew 24:22)

12. During the Great Tribulation, many false messiahs and false prophets will come.

The Lord Jesus warns his disciples the **second time** not to be deceived. Notice that this warning is given during the Great Tribulation – because of the global distress and persecution of Christians during that time, many Christians would arguably be looking for the appearing of the Lord Jesus to take them out of the world. Jesus tells his disciples not to be deceived by false messiahs and false prophets – which implies that even in the Great

Tribulation, the Lord Jesus still has not come. He says, *"At that time if anyone says to you, 'Look, here is the Messiah!' or, 'There he is!' do not believe it. For false messiahs and false prophets will appear and perform great signs and wonders to deceive, if possible, even the elect. See, I have told you ahead of time."* (Matthew 24:23-25)

It is noteworthy that Jesus gives the second warning about deceptions concerning his Second Coming **during** the Great Tribulation itself. This implies that he has not come yet, and only false messiah and false prophets will appear during this time to deceive many people. Notice that the Lord Jesus specifically says: *"See, I have told you ahead of time"*. Clearly, he was preparing his disciples – the Christians – for the future Tribulation ahead of time.

13. Jesus warns his disciples again about deception on his Second Coming – do not believe anyone who says he has come.

Jesus specifically warns his disciples not to believe anyone who says that he has come. Jesus says: *"So if anyone tells you, 'There he is, out in the wilderness,' do not go out; or, 'Here he is, in the inner rooms,' do not believe it."* (Matthew 24:26)

Notice that the only implication of this verse is that the Lord Jesus still has not come back to earth yet. And pre-tribulationists who say that Christ has already come to rapture the church would be directly contradicting this verse in the Bible where Jesus warns against spreading false rumors about his coming.

14. Jesus' Second Coming will be visible to all.

The Lord Jesus tells us that his Second Coming will be visible to all. The Apostle Paul tell us about the "splendor of his coming" which everyone on earth will see. Jesus says: "*For as lightning that comes from the east is visible even in the west, so will be the coming of the Son of Man. Wherever there is a carcass, there the vultures will gather.*" (Matthew 24:27-28)

15. The sun will be darkened and the stars will fall away.

Notice that before the coming of the Lord Jesus, Jesus tells us that "*immediately after the distress of those days, the sun will be darkened, and the moon will not give its light; the stars will fall from the sky, and the heavenly bodies will be shaken.*" (Matthew 24:29) Clearly, there will be events in the sky that plunges the whole world into darkness. It sets the stage for the arrival of Christ where the contrast between the darkness of the world and the splendor and brightness of his Second Coming is most apparent. In the Book of Zechariah, the prophet describes the day that the Lord Jesus comes as a unique day. He says, "*on that day there will be neither sunlight nor cold, frosty darkness. It will be a unique day – a day known only to the Lord – with no distinction between day and night.*" (Zechariah 14:6)

It is notable that the words "***immediately after** the distress of those days*" suggest that the coming of the Lord Jesus takes place after the Tribulation. When the sun is darkened, the moon does not give its light and the heavenly bodies are shaken, this the final sign before the actual coming of the Lord Jesus. Jesus tells his disciples, when you see all these things, you know that the end is near.

16. The Lord Jesus comes again on the clouds. The wicked world mourns at the coming of the Lord Jesus.

The Lord Jesus comes back to earth to reign with power and glory. He says: *"Then will appear the sign of the Son of Man in heaven. And then all the peoples of the earth will mourn when they see the Son of Man coming on the clouds of heaven, with power and great glory."* (Matthew 24:30) Notice that the Lord Jesus comes on the clouds – from the air – with great power and glory. His coming will be visible to everyone on earth. There is nothing secret about his coming.

17. The rapture of the saints occurs at the sound of the loud trumpet call.

The rapture of the saints occurs at the loud trumpet call. Jesus describes the rapture as follows: *"And he will send his angels with a **loud trumpet call**, and they will gather his elect from the four winds, from one end of the heavens to the other."* (Matthew 24:31) In the Gospel of Luke, Jesus tells his disciples: *"When these things begin to take place, stand up and lift up your heads, because your redemption is drawing near."* (Luke 21:28)

These verses describe the rapture of the elect from the ends of the earth. Notice that there is a **loud trumpet call** announcing the arrival of the Lord Jesus. And in 1 Thessalonians 4:16, the Apostle Paul tells us that *"the*

*Lord himself will come down from heaven, with a loud command, with the voice of the archangel and with the **trumpet call of God**, and the dead in Christ will rise first."*

It should be noted that the loud trumpet call is the single commonality announcing the arrival of the Lord Jesus, which is both mentioned in Matthew 24 and 1 Thessalonians 4:16. This suggests that the rapture is anything but secret. There will be a loud trumpet call announcing his arrival when Christ comes for his church. We will come to this point in more detail below.

There are several important observations from the three synoptic gospels on the Second Coming that I will highlight.

The Olivet Discourse in Matthew 24, Mark 13 and Luke 21 are addressed to Jesus' disciples – the Christians

One of the biggest questions that pre-tribulationists have to answer is who exactly is Matthew 24, Mark 13 and Luke 21 addressed to? According to them, since Christians have been raptured before the start of the Tribulation, it follows that these passages could only have been addressed to tribulation saints (i.e., unbelieving Jews and Gentiles who have turned to Christ during the Tribulation). John Walvoord in his book *The Rapture Question* writes that only tribulation saints, not the church-age Christians who have already been raptured, are to look for the signs of Jesus' coming. In his view, the present church-age Christians are to expect the Lord Jesus imminently, while the tribulation saints are to look for the signs of Jesus' coming during the Tribulation and then for the return of Christ to establish his kingdom.

Concerning the church and Christians in the present church-age, John Walvoord continues that they should expect Christ to return imminently to rapture them to heaven, and they are to get ready for an imminent rapture rather than to look for signs of Jesus' coming. Christians should therefore expect the rapture to occur at any moment. To defend his position on the pre-tribulation view, John Walvoord writes that *"the abandonment of the pretribulational return of Christ is tantamount to abandonment of the hope of His imminent return"*. (Walvoord, p. 75) Evidently, he thought that if Christians were to abandon the idea of an imminent rapture, this would be tantamount to abandoning the hope of Christ's imminent return.

Yet notice that at the very start of Luke 21, the idea of the imminency of Christ's return is exactly what the Lord Jesus warned us about. Jesus says:

> *"Watch out that you are not deceived. For many will come in my name, claiming, 'I am he,' and, **'The time is near'.***
> ***Do not follow them**."* (Luke 21:8) (*emphasis added*)

The Lord Jesus commands us to reject any notion that His return is imminent and tells us not to follow those who propagate such views that the end is near. Notice also that this command was given **before** the start of the Tribulation in verse 8, even before the verse on wars and rumors of wars in verse 9. It was the very first warning he gave at the start of the Olivet Discourse. Who was Jesus talking to before the start of the Tribulation? I believe he was talking to all Christians and not tribulation saints!

The very simple truth is that when Jesus gave the Olivet Discourse, he was speaking to his disciples – the Christians. In fact, Jesus goes on to tell his disciples about Great Tribulation:

> *"So when **you see standing in the holy place** 'the abomination that causes desolation,' spoken of through the prophet Daniel – let the reader understand – then let those who are in Judea flee to the mountains."* (Matthew 24:15) (*emphasis added*)

When Jesus said "*so when **you** see*" the abomination that causes desolation, he was clearly still talking to his disciples and not a separate group of Christians that had only recently come to believe in Christ during the Tribulation period. There is no evidence to suggest that Jesus was talking only to church-age Christians at the start of the Olivet Discourse (before mentioning the events of the Tribulation) and then only talking to tribulation saints in the middle of the discourse (when he talks about events during the Tribulation). He was clearly only addressing one crowd – his disciples –the Christians. The implication here is that all Christians, not just tribulation saints, will see the abomination that causes desolation and the Antichrist.

Similarly, the Apostle Paul tells the church in Thessalonica not to be deceived that the day of the Lord has already come. He says:

> *"Don't let anyone deceive you in any way, for that day will not come until the rebellion occurs and **the man of lawlessness is revealed**, the man doomed to destruction. He will oppose and will exact himself over everything that is called God or is worshipped, so that he sets himself*

up in God's temple, proclaiming himself to be God." (2 Thessalonians 2:3-4) (*emphasis added*)

Clearly, the Apostle Paul had in mind that the man of lawlessness must first be revealed before the day of the Lord, and the implication is that Christians should expect the man of lawlessness to be revealed first before Christ comes. If the church had already been raptured prior to the Tribulation and will not see the Antichrist, why would the Apostle Paul go to such lengths to tell Christians about the Antichrist? He might as well say, "Well, the day of the Lord has not yet come because you are still here!"

Notice where the warnings about deception concerning his Second Coming are given – one is pre-tribulation and the other during the Tribulation

It should be pointed out where the warnings about the deception of Jesus' Second Coming are given. The first warning is addressed right at beginning of the Olivet Discourse **before** the start of the Tribulation: *"Watch out that no one deceives you!"* (Matthew 24:4-5, Mark 13:5-6). The gospel of Luke goes even further – many will say *"'The time is near.' Do not follow them."* (Luke 21:8) (*emphasis added*) This is perhaps the clearest language from the Lord Jesus to reject those who say he is coming imminently. The implication raf giving these warnings before the start of the Tribulation is that Jesus is not coming before the Tribulation – he tells us that only false messiahs will come.

The second warning about the deception concerning his Second Coming is given **during** the Great Tribulation itself during the time of great distress, after the Antichrist has set himself up at the holy place (Matthew 24:23-25, Mark 13:22). Jesus tells us that the only kind of people appearing during that time will be false messiahs and false prophets – and if anyone tells others that the Messiah has come, they are by extension deceiving others. The implication of the second warning is that during the Great Tribulation, Christ has still not come yet!

Given that Jesus warns his disciples **before** and **during** the Tribulation to "watch and not be deceived", does this not suggest that Jesus has not yet come before and during the Tribulation?

By extension, if Jesus had already come to secretly rapture believers before the Tribulation with a loud trumpet call, it would be contrary to Jesus' command not to believe anyone who says he has come

The key point that I want to make here is that, if in fact Jesus had already come to secretly rapture the church before the Tribulation, this would be contrary to the command to his disciples not to believe anyone who says that Jesus has come (Matthew 24:4-5, Mark 13:5-6 and Luke 21:8). All three synoptic gospels state unequivocally that Jesus warns his disciples not to believe anyone who says that Jesus has come before and during the Tribulation – only false messiahs will appear – and it would be rather strange if Jesus had came with a loud trumpet call (1 Thessalonians 4:16) to rapture the church and then leave the tribulation saints behind with the warning that he has not come and not to be deceived.

I suspect that the pre-tribulation view is one the reasons why many people will be confused about Jesus' coming during the Tribulation – many will ask if they had been in fact left behind. Matthew 24:23-25 and Mark 13:22 are quite comforting to a believer who thinks he has been left behind if you read them carefully.

References to being flogged in "synagogues", and his warnings to those in Judea to flee, are addressed to Jewish believers. But other global events described in the Olivet Discourse are addressed to all Christians, both Jew and Gentile

It is true that the Lord Jesus specifically addresses believing Jews in some verses to prepare them for persecution – references to being flogged in the synagogues – and to flee from Judea when the Antichrist appears. He was after all addressing his disciples, who were Jewish.

I believe this reflects the Lord Jesus' concern not just for Gentile believers but also Jewish believers. There will be global events during the end times that affect all Christians (Gentile and Jewish) around the world – wars and rumors of wars (Matthew 24:6), famines and earthquakes (Matthew 24:7-8), universal persecution by all nations (Matthew 24:9), betrayal (Matthew 24:10-11), increase in wickedness in the world (Matthew 24:12-13), the preaching of the gospel to all nations (Matthew 24:14), calls to endure to the very end (Matthew 24:13), and the heavenly bodies will be shaken (Matthew 24:29).

However, there will be some events that take place in Israel that affect Jewish believers, such as the appearing of the Antichrist at the holy place (Matthew 24:15) and the call to flee from Judea (Matthew 24:17-20).

The Lord Jesus in all three synoptic gospels in Matthew 24, Mark 13 and Luke 21 told his disciples all the events that will come in the future to prepare both Gentile and Jewish believers for the Great Tribulation – and reflects his going concern for both Jewish and Gentile believers during the Tribulation when the Antichrist comes.

Nowhere in Matthew 24, Mark 13 and Luke 21 is there any mention of a rapture for Christians before the Tribulation

Finally, it should be noted that the Lord Jesus does not mention anything at all about a pre-tribulational rapture concerning Christians. It is odd that for such a monumental event affecting the church, Jesus says nothing about it. Jesus does in fact warn his disciples to watch and not be deceived before and during the Tribulation about his coming – so why would Jesus contradict himself and come secretly to rapture his church? If Jesus had in fact come to rapture Christians before the Tribulation, what is the purpose of Luke 21:8 to warn Christians before the Tribulation not to believe anyone who says the Messiah has come or that the end is near?

Furthermore, it is certainly quite dangerous to depart from the clear and natural words of Matthew 24, Mark 13 and Luke 21 concerning the Second Coming of Christ to read into them a secret rapture for Christians, when the primary intention of the Lord Jesus is to guard against deception. He tells his disciples: *"Watch out that no one deceives you."* And we should not be deceived likewise.

The error that pre-tribulationists make is to assume that the Olivet Discourse is directed solely at tribulation saints, when in fact it is directed to all Christians – including both Jew and Gentile Christians. The Lord Jesus warns his disciples about deception concerning his coming before and during the Tribulation. I do not think he was addressing tribulation saints because the first warning regarding the deception of his coming in Matthew 24:4-5, Mark 13:5-6 and Luke 21:8 was clearly given **before** the Tribulation. There is no evidence that Jesus intended the first half of the Olivet Discourse to be addressed to Christians and the second half to tribulation saints, nor does he make that distinction. The clear and natural meaning of the words in the Olivet Discourse point to the fact that all Christians – both Jew and Gentile – will have to go through the Tribulation and Christ comes **immediately after** the Tribulation (see Matthew 24:29, Mark 13:24).

The last loud trumpet call is the common feature announcing the arrival of Christ and the rapture of the church

It is clear from scripture that there will be a loud trumpet call when Christ comes on the clouds to rapture the church. In fact, the Apostle Paul describes the rapture and translation of saints to their glorified bodies as follows:

"Listen, I tell you a mystery: We will not all sleep, but we will all be changed – in a flash, in the twinkling of an eye, **at the last trumpet***. For the* **trumpet will sound***, the dead will be raised imperishable, and we will be changed."* (1 Corinthians 15:51-52) (*emphasis added*)

Notice that the Apostle Paul mentions that the dead will be raised imperishable at the "last trumpet" – not the second, third or fourth trumpet – but the very last one. And when Paul wrote to the Corinthians, he was clearly writing to believers – Christians – not tribulation saints.

Similarly in 1 Thessalonians 4:16-17, Paul mentions the trumpet call of God when writing to Christians, not tribulation saints, at Thessalonica:

"For the Lord himself will come down from heaven with a loud command, with the voice of the archangel and with the **trumpet call of God***, and the dead in Christ will rise first. After that, we who are still alive and are left will be caught up together with them in the clouds to meet the Lord in the air. And so we will be with the Lord forever."* (1 Thessalonians 4:16-17) (*emphasis added*)

And similarly in Matthew 24:31, the Lord Jesus himself tells us that there will be a loud trumpet call at the rapture of the saints:

"And he will send his angels with a **loud trumpet call***, and they will gather his elect from the four winds, from one end of the heavens to the other."* (Matthew 24:31) (*emphasis added*)

If we were to accept the pre-tribulationist position that Matthew 24:31 only refers to the gathering of tribulation saints and is a separate event from the rapture, then logically, in the pre-tribulationist mind, there must be not one but two loud trumpet calls because Paul tells the Christians in 1 Corinthians 15:51-52 and 1 Thessalonians 4:16-17 that there will be a loud trumpet call at the rapture.

However, there is not a single verse in the synoptic gospels where Jesus mentions two trumpet calls – one for the rapture and one for the gathering of tribulation saints. There is nothing in the Olivet Discourse in Matthew 24, Mark 13 or Luke 21 that talks about two separate trumpet calls. It would also be rather strange and confusing if the Lord Jesus announced his secret rapture to the world with a loud trumpet call, went back to heaven with the church, and then subsequently announced his final arrival to earth with another loud trumpet call. The Apostle Paul is clear in 1 Corinthians 15:51-52 that the rapture occurs at the "last trumpet". It is the very final event that occurs on the prophetic calendar where Jesus comes back to earth after the Tribulation, raptures the church and all Christians to meet him in the air, and comes back down to earth to reign as King with Christians.

#2 The character of our Lord Jesus

Part of the reason why pre-tribulationists often misconstrue the rapture and the Second Coming is the over-reliance on semantics. They tend to argue and debate about the meaning of certain words and phrases in scripture and interpret those words in a way that lends credence to their view. Much wasted ink has been spilled on debating the meaning of words such as "church", "elect", "saints", "caught up" and "gather" and whether these words meant the same thing or referred to different groups of people in different time periods or dispensations. If scripture cannot be read using its plain and natural meaning, I suppose then the Bible should have been written for scholars rather than ordinary people to understand.

It is quite pointless to debate about the meaning of words and semantics and ignoring the elephant in the room – the character of our Lord Jesus. What kind of person is the Lord Jesus? Is he the kind of person that takes people out of tribulation or have them to endure through it?

Consider the Lord Jesus' prayer before his crucifixion. He prays that Christians would not be taken out of the world but protected from the evil one. Furthermore, he prays that all who believe in his message will be one and brought to complete unity – whether Jew or Gentile:

> *"My prayer is **not that you take them out of the world** but you protect them from the evil one…my prayer is not for them alone, I pray also for those who will believe in me through their message, that **all of them may be one**…I have given them the glory that you gave me, that they may be one as we are one – I in them and you in me – so that they may be brought to complete unity."* (John 17:15-22) (*emphasis added*)

If the Lord Jesus prayed to keep Christians in the world, why would he change his mind and rapture all Christians out of the world before the Tribulation? I do not think that the Lord Jesus had in mind a pre-tribulational rapture when he prayed this prayer. Instead, he prayed for protection for all Christians from the evil one and for unity in his church that of them may be one. Notice that in his prayer, Jesus prayed that all Jews and Gentiles who believe in him should become one body in Christ – there is an emphasis on unity rather than on two separate peoples.

If I could take the semantic route as the pre-tribulationists like to do, I could argue that the word "protect" in John 17:15 is derived from the same Greek word (tērēsēs) that is used in Revelation 3:10 to "keep from" (tērēsō) the hour of trial. In other words, the Lord Jesus is asking not for Christians to be taken out of the world but to be protected and kept from the evil one. But none of the debate would be resolved by resorting purely to semantics as the meanings of words can be interpreted either way. This is why the Lord Jesus told his disciples:

> *"The Spirit gives life; the flesh counts for nothing. The words I have spoken to you – they are full of the Spirit and life. Yet there are some of you who do not believe...this is why I told you that no one can come to me unless the Father has enabled them."* (John 6:63-65)

Consider also the language that the Lord Jesus uses in Matthew 24:13 *"but the one who stands firm **to the end** will be saved."* The plain and natural meaning of the words "to the end" implies that Christians will have to endure the Tribulation to the end – Jesus promises the crown of life to those who overcome and not turn away from the faith. And in Luke 21:19, Jesus says, *"**Stand firm**, and you will win life."* None of these exhortations to stand firm and endure would make any sense if Christians are taken out of the big trouble – because how would Christians endure or stand firm if they are not there?

The Apostle Peter, whom the Lord Jesus told the kind of death he would experience in old age, wrote in 1 Peter 4:12 to Christians that they should expect suffering and persecution:

> *"Dear friends, do not be surprised at the **fiery ordeal** that has come on you to test you, as though something strange were happening to you. But rejoice inasmuch as you participate in the sufferings of Christ, so that you may be overjoyed when his glory is revealed."* (1 Peter 4:12) (*emphasis added*)

Clearly, Peter knew that Jesus was not coming imminently because Jesus had told him the kind of death he would die. He wrote that Christians are to patiently endure the "fiery ordeal" that is coming on them. I do not think Peter had in mind that Christians would have been raptured before the Tribulation when he wrote this letter; he clearly knew that Christians would face fiery trials and encouraged them to endure through it.

In the Book of Revelation, the Lord Jesus told Christians in the seven churches that he would reward the one who is "victorious". Notice that there is a consistent pattern here where Jesus rewards the victorious or the one who overcomes (i.e., to him that overcometh) if you use the King James Version of the Bible.

To the church in Ephesus, Jesus said:

> *"To the one who is **victorious**, I will give the right to eat from the tree of life, which is in the paradise of God."* (Revelation 2:7) (*emphasis added*)

To the church in Smyrna, Jesus said:

*"The one who is **victorious** will not be hurt at all by the second death."* (Revelation 2:8) (*emphasis added*)

To the church in Pergamum, Jesus said:

*"To the one who is **victorious**, I will give some of the hidden manna. I will also give that person a white stone with a new name written on it, known only to the one who receives it."* (Revelation 2:17) (*emphasis added*)

To the church in Thyatira, Jesus said:

*"To the one who is **victorious** and **does my will to the end**, I will give authority over the nations – that one 'will rule them with an iron scepter and will dash them to pieces like pottery – just as I have received authority from my Father. I will also give that one the morning star."* (Revelation 2:26-28) (*emphasis added*)

To the church in Sardis, Jesus said:

*"The one who is **victorious** will, like them, be dressed in white. I will never blot out the name of that person from the book of life, but will acknowledge that name before my Father and his angels."* (Revelation 3:5) (*emphasis added*)

To the church in Philadelphia, Jesus said:

*"To the one who is **victorious** I will make a pillar in the temple of my God. Never again will they leave it. I will write on them the name of my God and the name of the city of my God, the new Jerusalem, which is coming down out of heaven from my God; and I will also write on them my new name."* (Revelation 3:12) (*emphasis added*)

To the church in Laodicea, Jesus said:

> *"To the one who is **victorious**, I will give the right to sit with me on my throne, just as I was victorious and sat down with my Father on his throne."* (Revelation 3:21) (*emphasis added*)

Notice that in Jesus' message to all seven churches, he promises rewards to those who are victorious and does his will to the end seven times. If the churches are raptured before the Tribulation, how would they be victorious or said to have overcome? If Christians will be taken out of the world before the Tribulation comes, how would the sons of God be revealed?

It would be quite paradoxical for Jesus to promise Christians rewards for being victorious, for overcoming and to endure patiently, and then take them out of the world before the Tribulation begins.

Similarly, during the Tribulation when Christians will be killed and go into captivity, John writes *"this calls for patient endurance and faithfulness on the part of God's people"* (Revelation 13:10), which is consistent with the exhortations Jesus gives to the seven churches to endure and be victorious.

The Lord Jesus never promised Christians that he would take them out of trouble. In fact, he promised believers big trouble – he said, in this world you will have big trouble and persecution because the world hates you – but to the one who is victorious, overcomes and stands firm to the end, the Lord Jesus will reward him and acknowledge his name before the Father when he comes again.

#3 Jesus tells us that he is not coming imminently

The clearest scripture verse which shows that Jesus is not coming imminently is found in Luke's version of the Olivet Discourse. It is worth reproducing the scripture verses in full here:

> *"Teacher,", they asked, "when will these things happen? And what will be the sign that they are about to take place?" He replied: "Watch out that you are not deceived. For many will come in my name, claiming, 'I am he,' and, **'The time is near.' Do not follow them**."* (Luke 21:7-8) (*emphasis added*)

It should be noted that this warning not to be deceived is given even before the start of the Tribulation or before any of the events of the Tribulation are mentioned. The only implication from this verse is that Jesus is not coming pre-tribulation – only false messiahs will come – and any teaching that Christ is coming imminently or that the time of his coming is near should be rejected. Jesus tells us bluntly – many will claim that "the time is near" – do not follow them.

The fact that this warning is deliberately given **before** the start of the Tribulation should be a sobering thought for pre-tribulationists who say that Jesus is coming imminently or at any moment because by implication of Luke 21:7-8, they are deceiving others. John Walvoord wrote that *"the abandonment of the pretribulational return of Christ is tantamount to abandonment of the hope of His imminent return."* (Walvoord, p. 75) To a certain extent, John Walvoord is right that we should abandon the hope of an imminent return. The Lord Jesus himself tells us that he is not coming imminently – and he then goes on to tell us the parable of the wicked servant, the parable of the ten virgins and the parable of the bags of gold where the single commonality is that the bridegroom or master was a "long time coming". The true test, as Jesus suggests, is not what you would do if you thought your master was coming tomorrow, but if he was gone away for a long time or not returning even in your lifetime. Would you remain faithful and true, or would you become wicked and complacent? We will elaborate on this in more detail below.

Immediately after the Olivet Discourse, the Lord Jesus gives his disciples the lesson from the fig free. He says:

> *"Now learn this lesson from the fig free: As soon as its twigs get tender and its leaves come out, you know that summer is near. Even so, when you see all these things, you know that it is near, right at the door. Truly I tell you, this generation will certainly not pass away until all these things have happened."* (Matthew 24:32-33)

The meaning of these words should be clear that Jesus was talking about the signs of his Second Coming – and once you see the signs as described in Matthew 24 such as the appearing of the Antichrist in the holy place and the sun refusing to give its light (i.e., when the heavenly bodies are shaken), you know that Jesus is right at the door, ready to come back to earth to establish his kingdom. The only implication of such a verse is that Jesus is not coming imminently unless these signs have been fulfilled first.

Yet, there are some pre-tribulationists including Hal Lindsey who viewed the establishment of Israel as a nation as the fulfillment of the "fig free" passage in Matthew 24:32-33. Lindsey contends that the leaves of the fig tree unfurled on May 14, 1948 when Israel became a nation and a new "generation" of Jews will see the rebirth of Israel.

This is a classic illustration of pre-tribulationists taking verses out of context – which is why it is so important to consider verses from the other synoptic gospels to get a clearer context of what Jesus was saying. For example, regarding the fig tree, Luke's gospel tells us that Jesus said:

> *"Look at the fig tree and **all the trees**. When they sprout leaves, you can see for yourselves and know that summer is near. Even so, when you see these things happening, you know that the kingdom of God is near."* (Luke 21:29-31) (*emphasis added*)

Clearly, Jesus was not referring to a single fig tree (which Hal Lindsey thought represented Israel) but to all the trees. And Jesus tells his disciples, when you see all the trees sprouting leaves, you know that summer is near. It is an extremely simple analogy to look for the signs of his coming. When you **see** the signs, you know that he is very near. These signs were meant to be visible for all to see.

Now the next practical question we should ask is, have the signs of Jesus' coming been fulfilled? The answer is that we are probably still in the beginning of birth pains – where there are wars and rumors of wars, nation rising against nation, kingdom against kingdom, famines and earthquakes in various places. We see signs of these things happening in the world right now in the modern age.

The rest of the signs such as universal persecution of Christians, increase in wickedness in the world and preaching the gospel to all nations have not been fulfilled yet – even though we see localized persecution of Christians in certain continents such as Africa and the Middle East. Jesus tells us that Christians must first be hated by all nations and there will be universal persecution.

The final signs such as the appearing of the Antichrist in the holy place and celestial events in the sky (i.e., the darkening of the sun and moon, and stars falling from the sky) have not taken place at all. Jesus tells us that when you see these signs, you know that he is coming very soon. The key phrase he uses is **"*Immediately after* the distress of those days...**" (Matthew 24:29) (*emphasis added*) which indicates that Jesus is coming after the Tribulation.

Pre-tribulationists, however, argue that Matthew 24 was written for tribulation saints and not to the church – because in their view, the church would have been already raptured. Therefore, according to them, only tribulation saints are to watch for the signs of his Second Coming. They point to verses such as Matthew 24:42: "*Therefore keep watch, because you do not know on what day your Lord will come*" and Matthew 24:44: "*So you also must be ready, because the Son of Man will come at an hour when you do not expect him*" as evidence that Jesus is coming imminently for the church and we will not know the day and hour Jesus will come.

I believe the pre-tribulationists are mistaken. It is true that we will not know the actual day and hour that Jesus will come (not even the Lord Jesus knows – only the Father), but the exhortation here is to watch for the signs of his coming so that when you see the signs, you know that Jesus is coming very soon, even though you do not know the day or hour. The fact that we do not know the day and hour does not *ipso facto* mean that Jesus is coming imminently.

Let's take an analogy of a volcano. A volcanologist may not be able to predict the exact day and hour the volcano will erupt, but he may be able to tell you the signs that show a volcano may erupt soon. Some of the notable signs that an eruption might take place soon include an increase in the frequency and intensity of felt earthquakes, noticeable steaming or enlarged areas of hot ground, or swelling on the ground surface and changes in heat flow. The volcanologist may not be able to tell you exactly what date the volcano will erupt; but the one who keeps watch will know the signs and observe that the volcano will be erupting very soon (the obvious sign being smoke coming out from the volcano) and possibly tell the people in surrounding areas to get ready or evacuate before it does erupt. The mere fact that we do not know the day and hour that the volcano will erupt does not mean that it should erupt imminently, especially if the volcano looks to be dormant at the moment.

Pre-tribulationists like to point to the fact that "*the Son of Man will come at an hour when you do not expect him*", and therefore Christians would not expect Jesus when he comes. However, if you read this passage in Matthew carefully, Jesus went on to tell his disciples a parable of a lazy and wicked servant who thinks to himself that his master is staying away for a long time. He says:

> "*But suppose that servant is wicked and says to himself,*
> '***My master is staying away a long time***,' *and he then*

*begins to beat his fellow servants and to eat and drink with drunkards. **The master of that servant will come on a day when he does not expect him and at an hour he is not aware of.** He will cut him to pieces and assign him a place with the hypocrites, where there will be weeping and gnashing of teeth.*" (Matthew 24:48-51) (*emphasis added*)

The key point that the Lord Jesus is making here is **not** that he comes at an hour that watchful Christians would not expect him, but rather he comes at an hour that a wicked and lazy servant would not expect him. The lazy servant who has no regard for his master and who probably does not read the Bible will not recognize the signs of his coming, because he does not know what to look for and does not care. The wise servant, however, will be keeping watch and will recognize the signs of the Lord's coming. The only kind of people that will be caught by surprise are those who have neglected to keep watch and repent. Watchful Christians that recognize the signs of Jesus' coming will not be caught by surprise. The element of surprise is reserved for those who have fallen asleep and do not see the signs of his coming (i.e., those who are wicked and do not know God's word).

Similarly, in the Book of Revelation, the Lord Jesus tells the church in Sardis:

*"Remember, therefore, what you have received and heard; hold it fast, and repent. **But if you do not wake up, I will come like a thief**, and you will not know at what time I will come to you.*" (Revelation 3:3) (*emphasis added*)

In other words, the Lord Jesus only comes like a thief to those who have not repented and to those who remain asleep in their faith and would thus not recognize the signs of his coming. The Lord Jesus will not come like a thief to Christians who are keeping watch for him because they are prepared and recognize the signs of his coming. Jesus' will only come like a thief to the church in Sardis if they do not wake up – the words "but if" suggest that Jesus' coming like a thief is the consequence of the church in Sardis not waking up and repenting.

It is noteworthy that immediately after the Olivet Discourse, the Lord Jesus then told his disciples the parable of the ten virgins. In that parable, Jesus specifically mentions his coming was not imminent. He says:

> *"The bridegroom was a **long time in coming**, and they all became drowsy and fell asleep."* (Matthew 25:5) (*emphasis added*)

In this parable, notice that the Lord Jesus did not say he was coming imminently. Rather, the emphasis is that he will be gone for a long time. Jesus will catch Christians who are unprepared by surprise, but those who are ready and expecting him will keep watch and not be surprised at his coming because they recognize the signs of his coming.

Jesus then repeats this point in the parable of the bags of gold. He says:

> *"Again, it will be like a man going on a journey, who called his servants and entrusted his wealth to them...**after a long time** the master of those servants returned and settled accounts with them."* (Matthew 25:14-19) (*emphasis added*)

I do not think the intention of these verses convey that Jesus' coming is imminent in the sense that it can occur at any moment now. He clearly tells his disciples that he will take a long time to come, and the key point here is to keep watch and be ready for his coming. Jesus certainly did not convey the kind of message that he was coming tomorrow or at any moment as some Christians would like to have it – he will be coming after a long time and he was guarding against Christians becoming complacent and not keeping watch for the signs of his coming in the fig tree analogy. The element of surprise is only reserved for unbelievers or for Christians who are asleep in their faith and who do not know the Word of God.

This is not to say that the Lord Jesus' coming will always be not imminent. There will come a time in the future when Jesus' coming will be truly imminent and watchful Christians will know that he is near by looking at the signs, so that they will not be taken by surprise when he comes, just as how one might observe a dormant volcano becoming active in the future.

I agree with David Pawson that the true test is not what you would do if you thought Jesus was coming tomorrow, but rather what you would do if Jesus was not coming in the next 1,000 years. Would you continue to stay faithful and true to the Word of God even though you know Jesus is not coming in your lifetime? And I believe the references to keeping watch and being awake in these verses are aimed precisely at the kind of complacency that the Lord Jesus was guarding against in the interim before he comes again.

If you believe that the Lord Jesus is coming imminently or tomorrow, it will have a profound effect on the way you live your life. A person who thinks Jesus is coming tomorrow or at any moment might not want to go to bed with his wife tonight, thinking that Jesus might come while he was still in bed making love and catching him in the act. Or he might not want to go to work the next day, because why should you work if Jesus might come imminently or at any moment and rapture you to heaven?

The church in Thessalonica suffered from precisely the same tragic consequence of truly believing that Christ was coming imminently. They had earlier received a report allegedly from Paul asserting that the day of the Lord had already come (2 Thessalonians 2:2). The result was that people in the church had started to become idle and stopped working, because they thought that Jesus would come at any moment. Paul writes:

> *"In the name of the Lord Jesus Christ, we command you, brothers and sisters, to keep away from every believer who is idle and disruptive and does not live according to the teaching you received from us. For you yourselves know how you ought to follow our example. We were not idle when we were with you, nor did we eat anyone's food without paying for it."* (2 Thessalonians 3:6-8)

This is why the Apostle Paul tells the believers in Thessalonica that the man of lawlessness must first appear before the day of the Lord comes. He was clearly referring to the sign that Jesus gave about the abomination that causes desolation appearing in the holy place. Since these events have not taken place yet, the day of the Lord could not have arrived. Paul then goes on by admonishing the church in Thessalonica to settle down and go back to work, and not to associate with members who are idle and disruptive, warning them to return to the truth of the gospel as a fellow believer.

Paul's second letter to the Thessalonians is therefore a real-life case study of the consequence of believing that Christ is coming imminently – and actually taking it seriously. People start to quit their jobs and become idle, since in their minds they think, "Well, if Christ is coming tomorrow, why should I work?" And Paul had the task of admonishing them: "*The one who is unwilling to work shall not eat.*" (2 Thessalonians 3:10)

David Pawson, in his sermon on "*Israel, the Church in the End Times*" in Conference in Kansas City, USA, said:

> "*I had to counsel a lovely young lady, who spent all her spare time in the cemetery where her parents are buried, hour after hour, because she wanted to be caught up with her father and mother. That's neurotic. And I had to help her out of that. We are not to be watching the clouds, we are to be watching the signs on earth of his coming. We need to pray for insight and pray that we will not be deceived.*"

I believe that likewise, we should not be deceived that Christ's coming is imminent but rather, we should watch for the signs of his coming as set out in Matthew 24 and reiterated in the other synoptic gospels. We should not be living our lives watching the clouds in expectancy of Christ's imminent return. It is very interesting to note that the Lord Jesus himself tells us that only when all the signs of his coming are fulfilled, only then should we look up at the clouds. He says:

> "*And when these things begin to come to pass, **then look up**, and lift up your heads; for your redemption draweth nigh.*" (Luke 21:28 KJV) (*emphasis added*)

In other words, only when all the signs of his coming have been fulfilled and when we see the sign of the Son of Man in the clouds – only then should we look up in expectancy of Christ's imminent return.

Pre-tribulationists may counter and say, "Well, to abandon the hope that Christ is coming imminently would make Christians complacent", but they fail to realize that the opposite is also true – as the church in Thessalonica demonstrated – people can start to become idle and disruptive. I believe the Lord Jesus told us about these parables precisely because he was looking for believers that are truly faithful servants – rather than people who serve him because they are in "panic mode" that Christ is coming imminently or at any moment.

#4 Paul's true intention when he wrote to the Thessalonians

Pre-tribulationists often quote scripture verses from 1 Thessalonians and 2 Thessalonians to support their view that Christ is coming imminently and will rapture all Christians out of the world before the Tribulation. They refer to 1 Thessalonians 4:16-18 describing the rapture and the phrase *"therefore encourage one another with these words"* that Paul uses as the basis that Christians will be raptured from the coming wrath. It is worth reproducing these scripture verses in full here:

> *"For the Lord himself will come down from heaven, with a loud command, with the voice of the archangel and with the trumpet call of God, and the dead in Christ will rise first. After that, we who are still alive and are left will be*

> *caught up together with them in the clouds to meet the Lord in the air. And so we will be with the Lord forever.* ***Therefore encourage one another with these words***." (1 Thessalonians 4:16-18) (*emphasis added*)

Pre-tribulationists argue that the purpose of the rapture is to take Christians out of the world before the Tribulation and to avoid the coming wrath – otherwise why would Paul ask Christians to encourage one another with these words? According to them, the implication of encouraging one another is to give each other hope that they will escape the coming wrath on earth.

However, this is where I believe pre-tribulationists are mistaken as to the Apostle Paul's true intentions in writing to the Thessalonians. To truly understand the context of this letter, we need to look at the reason why Paul wrote to the Thessalonians. In other words, what is the purpose of Paul's letter to the Thessalonians? What was the issue he was trying to address in Thessalonica at that historical point in time?

Once we understand the historical context underpinning Paul's letters to the Thessalonians, we start to get a clearer picture why Paul wrote certain things to the Thessalonians in response to the issues that plagued the church in that historical period in ancient Greece. So for example, Paul writes in 1 Thessalonians 4:3-8 on the issue of sexual immorality because it was a rampant issue at that time. Sexual immorality was in fact, so rampant and so out of control, that it was even regarded as acceptable in society for men to have affairs and frequent prostitutes.

In his book *Exploring 1 & 2 Thessalonians*, John Phillips describes that *"Greek culture gave wide approval to all forms of sexual misbehavior.*" (Philips, p. 100) In his view, the idea that extramarital sex was morally wrong was quite foreign to the Greek way of thinking. Greek wives were expected to be chaste, mothers of children and keepers of the household, while Greek husbands could do as they pleased and have extramarital affairs with concubines and prostitutes. They did this "*with the full approval of society.*" (Philips, p. 100) John Phillips notes that conventional morality at that time did not see anything wrong with having extramarital affairs and engaging in all kinds of sexual misbehavior. In the Book of Romans, we find the Apostle Paul describing the situation where "*God gave them over to shameful lusts*" (Romans 1:26-27) where men and women exchanged natural sexual relations and were inflamed with lust for one another.

Similarly, John R. W. Stott, the preeminent scholar on the subject, wrote in his book *The Gospel & the End of Time: The Message of 1 & 2 Thessalonians (1991)* that sexual immorality was especially rampant in both Corinth and Thessalonica. He writes that Thessalonica "*was particularly associated with the worship of deities called the Cabiri, in whose rites gross immorality was promoted under the name of religion.*" (Stott, p. 81) However, John Stott notes that sexual immorality in the Roman empire was so rampant that he doubted if Corinth or Thessalonica were any worse than other cities during that time period.

Clearly, the Apostle Paul was very concerned about sexual immorality within the church in Thessalonica. And the reason why he wrote part of the letter on sexual immorality was because he was trying to address the evil that was going on in the church in Thessalonica at that time. It is not difficult to see that the

Apostle Paul was writing to the Thessalonians in response to something that he had heard, most likely from Timothy (1 Thessalonians 3:6).

Now concerning the rapture – one has to really take a step back and ask – why did the Apostle Paul write about the rapture to the Thessalonians? What was the evil he was trying to address at that particular time in Thessalonica? The answer is that it lies in part towards the Greek world's attitude towards death at that time.

In the ancient Greek world, it was common to think that death was the end of everything and there was no concept of the resurrection. Aeschylus, the ancient Greek tragedian, described the concept of death in his play "The Eumenidies", where Apollo remarks: "*Once a man has died, and the dust has soaked up his blood, there is no resurrection.*" Theocritus, the ancient Greek poet from Sicily, wrote: "*There is hope for those who are alive, but those who have died are without hope.*" Similarly, Catullus, the Latin poet of the late Roman Republic, wrote in Catullus 5 in an ode to Lesbia "*once the brief light [of life] has set, an eternal night [of death] must be slept.*" In other words, the Greeks thought that death was eternal and a permanent state – there was no such thing as a resurrection in the Greek mind.

Apparently, some members of the church in Thessalonica thought that once they had died, there was no way of seeing Jesus when he came back to earth because they would remain in a permanent state of death. They thought those who had died had missed the Second Coming of Christ and therefore thought that those church members who had died had missed the resurrection.

This is precisely why in 1 Thessalonians 4:13, Paul writes to the Thessalonians not to be "***uninformed about those who sleep in death***, *so that you do not grieve like the rest of mankind,* ***who have no hope***." (*emphasis added*) The idea of the dead having no hope and no resurrection was prevalent Greek thinking during that time period, and it is not surprising that members of the church in Thessalonica thought that those who had died had no more hope because they missed the resurrection. Paul goes on to then say:

> "***According to the Lord's word***, *we tell you that we who are still alive, who are left until the coming of the Lord,* ***will certainly not precede those who have fallen asleep***. *For the Lord himself will come down from heaven, with a loud command, with the voice of the archangel and with the trumpet call of God, and the* ***dead in Christ will rise first***. *After that, we who are still alive and are left will be caught up together with them in the clouds to meet the Lord in the air. And so we will be with the Lord forever.* ***Therefore encourage one another with these words.***" (1 Thessalonians 4:15-18) (*emphasis added*)

Notice that Paul's intention in this verse is to tell the church in Thessalonica that those who have died are not "left behind" – in fact, they are given the front row seat because the dead in Christ will rise first. This is why Paul says that those who are alive will certainly not precede those who have fallen asleep. And Paul goes on to say "*therefore encourage one another with these words*" – in other words – those members of the church who have already died are not "left behind" but will partake in the Second Coming of Christ. They will be raised first when Jesus comes. Paul is effectively telling the Thessalonians that death does not mean that they will miss out on the Second Coming and to encourage one another that there is a resurrection for the dead – unlike the rest of mankind who have no hope.

Notice also that Paul says "according to the Lord's word" – which suggests that he derived this based on what the Lord Jesus said about his Second Coming. The only time Jesus spoke about his Second Coming in detail is found in the Olivet Discourse in Matthew 24, Mark 13 and Luke 21 where he also mentions the "trumpet" call announcing his coming.

More significantly, there is no mention of "wrath" whatsoever in 1 Thessalonians 4. Paul's intention, taken in the historical context of Thessalonica and Greek thinking at that time, was simply trying to address the concern that those who had died had no hope (1 Thessalonians 4:13) and will not partake in the Second Coming of Christ. Therefore, Paul says, encourage each other with these words – precisely because those who had died in Christ will be raised and have a front row seat at the Second Coming. I believe pre-tribulationists are badly mistaken on this point of encouragement as a deliverance from wrath; rather, it is Paul's intention to encourage members of the church that the dead would not miss out on the resurrection and the Second Coming.

Pre-tribulationists may counter and say, "Well, subsequently in 1 Thessalonians 5:2, Paul goes on to say that the day of the Lord will come like a thief in the night, and in 1 Thessalonians 5:9, Paul tells them that God did not appoint us to suffer wrath." Does this not connote an element of surprise when the day of the Lord comes? Wouldn't Christians be spared from God's wrath? Let's examine these scripture verses in detail:

"Now, brothers and sisters, about times and dates we do not need to write to you, for you know very well that the day of the **Lord will come like a thief in the night***. While people are saying, "Peace and safety", destruction will come on them suddenly, as labour pains on a pregnant woman, and they will not escape." (1 Thessalonians 5:1-3) (emphasis added)*

Pre-tribulationists like to quote this verse to say that the day of the Lord comes suddenly – and there will be an element of surprise when that day comes. Notice however, that Paul immediately goes on to say:

"But you, brothers and sisters, **are not in darkness so that this day should surprise you like a thief***. You are all children of the light and children of the day.* **We do not belong to night** *or to the darkness." (1 Thessalonians 5:4) (emphasis added)*

The key point that the Apostle Paul is making here is that Christians do not belong to the night or to the darkness where the Lord will come like a thief. There is a stark contrast between those who live in darkness and those who live in the light – and Paul says, you are not in darkness so that this day should surprise you like a thief. In other words, Paul is saying that Christians will not be caught off guard by the day of the Lord because we are in the light – we know God's word and the signs of his coming – watchful Christians who are sober and awake will be fully prepared for it.

I believe the contrast between the thief in the "night" and Christians – who are all children of the "light" and children of the "day" is rather telling regarding Paul's intentions. Clearly, he meant that children of the **light** and of the **day** will not be surprised or caught off guard when the day of the Lord comes suddenly like a thief in the **night**. But the world, which lives in darkness, will be caught off guard. Paul describes this day of the Lord as "labor pains on a pregnant woman" which comes suddenly – but watchful Christians will not be caught by surprise when it comes because they belong to the day and know the signs of his coming.

Paul then goes on to say one of the most heavily quoted verses by pre-tribulationists to support the view that Christians will be taken out of the Tribulation. He says:

> *"But since we belong to the day, let us be sober, putting on faith and love as a breastplate, and hope of salvation as a helmet.* ***For God did not appoint us to suffer wrath*** *but to receive salvation through our Lord Jesus Christ. He died for us so that, whether we are awake or* ***asleep****, we may live together with him. Therefore* ***encourage one another and build each other up****, just as in fact you are doing."* (1 Thessalonians 5:8-11) (*emphasis added*)

Pre-tribulationists argue that since God did not appoint Christians to suffer wrath, they will therefore be raptured out of the world before the Tribulation comes, and Christians are to encourage one another with these words.

It is quite interesting to note that at the beginning of 1 Thessalonians 5, the Apostle Paul tells the church that they "*are not in darkness, so that this day should surprise you like a thief*". He then goes on to mention the pieces of armor that a solider would put on to get ready for battle, such as a "breastplate" and "helmet". I would just pause here for a moment to say that it would be rather odd if Paul's intention was to tell the church that they would not be surprised when the day of the Lord comes, and to put on the "breastplate" of faith and love and "helmet" of hope of salvation, and immediately tells them that they would not be there when the day of the Lord comes. References to not being "surprised", "children of the day", "breastplate" and "helmet", like a well-informed solider going into battle, are not the kind of words that one would use if Christians were not going into the day of the Lord that comes like a thief in the "night" on the whole world.

I believe Paul meant something else when he said, *"For God did not appoint us to suffer wrath"*, because the very next words he used are *"but to **receive salvation through our Lord Jesus Christ**."* The implication here is that one who does not receive salvation through our Lord Jesus Christ will be under God's wrath. And this is true – the lake of fire – is the ultimate expression of God's wrath where he will cast unbelievers who have rejected Christ. The point that the Apostle Paul was making here was on salvation through the Lord Jesus, rather than escape from the coming Tribulation.

It is very telling that Paul goes on in the next sentence to say *"He died for us, so that, whether we are awake or **asleep**, we may live together with him."* Those Christians who have died are clearly not going to experience the Tribulation or the day of the Lord, so why does Paul mention them? The answer is because those Christians who have died will not be consigned to the lake of fire but will live together with Christ. The intention of this verse is a reiteration that the salvation we have in Jesus saves us from eternal wrath. And Paul goes on to say, *"Therefore encourage one another and build each other up."* Remember at the beginning of this chapter, we mentioned that the church in Thessalonica was plagued by the Greek thinking that there was no resurrection and death was the end. Paul was telling the Thessalonians that death was not the end – whether we are dead or alive – Christ died for us so that we may live together with him.

Let's do a test if Paul's intention here was really a rapture from the wrath of God. Suppose we substituted the phrase *"For God did not appoint us to suffer wrath"* with *"For God did not appoint us to go through the day of the Lord"* – how would this look in the context of verses 4-11? It would look like this:

"But you, brothers and sisters, are not in darkness so that this day should surprise you like a thief...But since we belong to the day, let us be sober, putting on faith and love as a breastplate, and the hope of salvation as a helmet. ***For God did not appoint us to go through the day of the Lord*** *but to receive salvation through our Lord Jesus Christ. He died for us so that, whether we are awake or asleep, we may live together with him."*

It would be quite apparent that, once we substitute "God's wrath" for "the day of the Lord", it does not fit with Paul's intention in verse 4 that this day should not surprise you like a thief, as well as putting on faith and love as a breastplate and hope of salvation as a helmet. It seems counter intuitive that Paul would mention the breastplate and helmet and suddenly in the next verse, mention that God did not appoint us to go through the day of the Lord or the Tribulation. Why then the need for a breastplate and helmet, which are the armor a solider puts on before going into battle?

God's wrath, in the context of these verses, must be read together in the context with receiving salvation from the Lord Jesus. Those who do not receive salvation will indeed be under God's wrath in the sense of an eternal judgment – this is the real point that the Apostle Paul was driving at. Christians have the "hope of salvation as a helmet", just as a soldier goes in prepared on the day of battle, knowing that if he dies, his salvation in Christ is assured. It becomes even more apparent, when we examine Paul's letter in 2 Thessalonians, that Christians are to go through the Tribulation.

In 2 Thessalonians, we find the opposite scenario where the church in Thessalonica received a report, allegedly from Paul, that the day of the Lord had already come. The consequence of believing such as report were that certain members in the church in Thessalonica started to become idle and disruptive (2 Thessalonians 3:6). Paul's response to the Thessalonians is noteworthy:

> *"Don't let anyone deceive you in any way, **for that day will not come until the rebellion occurs and the man of lawlessness is revealed**, the man doomed to destruction. He will oppose and will exalt himself over everything that is called God or is worshipped, so that he sets himself up in God's temple, proclaiming himself to be God."* (2 Thessalonians 2:3-4) (*emphasis added*)

Notice that Paul says that the day of the Lord cannot come unless the "rebellion" occurs first and the "man of lawlessness is revealed". What is this rebellion and the man of lawlessness? I believe that Paul was clearly referring to the universal persecution of Christians and the Antichrist who sets up the "abomination that causes desolation" in the holy place (Matthew 24:15). The Book of Daniel records this event as follows:

> *"He will confirm a covenant with many for one seven. In the middle of the 'seven' he will put an end to sacrifice and offering. And at the temple he will set up an abomination that causes desolation, until the end that is decreed is poured out on him."* (Daniel 9:27)

Clearly, Paul was telling the church in Thessalonica that the day of the Lord had not come yet because the man of lawlessness had not been revealed. It is noteworthy that the first admonishment to the Thessalonians in these verses is not to be deceived – which is exactly the kind of warning that the Lord Jesus gives his disciples in the Olivet Discourse. The obvious implication is that there is going to be a lot of deception going around concerning the Second Coming of Christ and the Great Tribulation. Paul goes on to say:

> *"And then the lawless one will be revealed, whom the Lord Jesus will overthrow with the breath of his mouth and* **destroy by the splendor of his coming***. The coming of the lawless one will be in accordance with how Satan works. He will use all sorts of display of power through signs and wonders that serve the lie, and all the ways that wickedness deceives those who are perishing. They perish because they refused to love the truth and so be saved."* (2 Thessalonians 2:8) (*emphasis added*)

The implication of these verses is that the man of lawlessness must first be revealed before Christ comes – and Paul says that the lawless one will be destroyed by the splendor of his coming. Notice that when Christ comes, it will be a glorious and splendorous coming. The coming of the lawless one will be marked by all kinds of deception including all sorts of display of power through signs and wonders that serve the lie – the lie that he is God. This is why the Apostle Paul then goes on to tell the Thessalonians to stand firm and hold fast to the teachings of scripture. He says:

*"So then, brothers and sisters, **stand firm** and **hold fast** to the teachings we passed on to you, whether by word of mouth or by letter."* (2 Thessalonians 2:15) (*emphasis added*)

It should be rather straightforward to see that the Apostle Paul, having warned them about the deception of the Antichrist, tells the church in Thessalonica to stand firm and hold fast to the teachings that they had been given. He was clearly telling them to be strong in the faith and not to be deceived.

I would pause here to note that the exhortations to stand firm and hold fast to the teachings, and the warnings about deception, would not really make any sense if the church was going to be raptured before the Tribulation comes and the man of lawlessness is revealed. If the church had already been raptured out of the world before the Tribulation, then what is the purpose of giving all the details about the deception of the Antichrist – signs and wonders that serve the lie – to the church in Thessalonica? It would have been of no practical use to them. Paul's intention in telling the church to stand firm and hold fast to the teachings is precisely because there will be a lot of deception when the Antichrist comes – Jesus tells us that the Antichrist and false prophet will perform *"signs and wonders to deceive, if possible, even the elect."* (Matthew 24:24)

Paul then tells the church in 2 Thessalonians 3:6 not to be idle. Apparently, some had believed the report that the day of the Lord had come and thought that Jesus' coming was imminent. As a result they started to become idle and disruptive because they thought, if Christ is coming tomorrow, why should I continue to work?

The pre-tribulationist position that Christ is coming imminently or at any moment is precisely the kind of doctrine that the Apostle Paul was guarding against in his second letter to the Thessalonians. When people actually take seriously the fact that Christ may come at any moment, they start to quit their jobs and become idle. Paul's instruction to watch for the revealing of the man of lawlessness is consistent with Jesus' Olivet Discourse to watch for the signs of his coming. The implication is that Christ will not come unless the man of lawlessness is first revealed first.

Pre-tribulationists argue that to abandon the pre-tribulation position would be tantamount to abandoning the hope of Christ's imminent return. I do believe that we should abandon the hope of Christ's imminent return in the sense that the signs of his coming have not yet come to fruition. However, the mere fact that Christ may not return in our lifetime does not mean that we will not be with Christ. This is precisely why Paul encourages the church in Thessalonica in 1 Thessalonians 5:10: *"He died* *for us so that, whether we are awake or **asleep**, we may live together with him. Therefore encourage one another and build each other up, just as in fact you are doing.*" Clearly, he was addressing the concerns of the church that those who had died would have missed out on Christ's coming – and he tells us that those who have died will not miss out when Christ comes – we will get a front row seat when the rapture occurs: "*the dead in Christ will rise first*".

The appropriate response to pre-tribulationists who say that we are abandoning the hope of Christ's imminent return is therefore – in the words of the Apostle Paul – that whether we are awake or asleep, we will live together with Christ. Death does not mean we will miss out on the resurrection or the Second Coming. Therefore encourage each other with these words.

The church in Thessalonica is a real-life case study of what happens when people actually start to take the imminent return of Christ very seriously. The pre-tribulationists may argue, well, to preach that Christ is not returning imminently would make Christians complacent in their faith. However, the real test as Jesus suggests, is not what you would do if you thought your master was coming back tomorrow, but what you would do if your master was a **long time coming**. This is the true test of whether a servant is faithful and not simply in the faith because of the "panic" that he feels that Christ may come imminently back to earth. Jesus asks: "*Who then is the wise and faithful servant?*" (Matthew 24:45) – and we should pause and consider carefully what Jesus meant by these words.

#5 The Revelation was given to prepare Christians for the Tribulation in the future

If there is anything we learn about the character of our Lord Jesus, it is that he prepares Christians ahead of time for the fiery trial and persecution that they will face on account of his name. When one reads the Olivet Discourse in Matthew 24, Mark 13 and Luke 21 carefully, it becomes apparent that whole purpose of the Olivet Discourse is to prepare Christians for tribulation ahead of time. Jesus says: ***"See, I have told you ahead of time."*** (Matthew 24:25) (*emphasis added*)

It is very like Jesus to warn us and tell us what must take place in the future so that we can prepare ahead of time. At the beginning of the Book of Revelation, John writes: *"The revelation from Jesus Christ, which God gave him to show his servants what must soon take place. He made it known by sending his angel to his servant John, who testifies to everything he saw – that is, the word of God and the testimony of Jesus Christ."* (Revelation 1:1-2) Clearly, the Lord Jesus gave John the Revelation and his testimony to prepare his servants – the Christians – for what must take place in the future.

Surprisingly, pre-tribulationists argue that Revelation 4-18 do not concern church-age Christians because they would have been raptured before the Tribulation. To support this argument, they claim that the Tribulation period described in Revelation concerns only Israel and unsaved believers. Daniel's seventieth week therefore only concerns the nation of Israel (i.e., unsaved Jews) which should not be confused with the church. Let's take a look at the verse concerning Daniel's seventieth week:

> *"Seventy 'sevens' are decreed for **your people** and **your
> holy city** to finish transgression, to put an end to sin, to atone
> for wickedness, to bring in everlasting righteousness, to
> seal up vision and prophecy and to anoint the Most Holy
> Place."* (Daniel 9:24) (*emphasis added*)

Pre-tribulationists argue that since these prophetic verses concern "your people" (i.e., the Jews) and "your holy city" (i.e., Jerusalem), it therefore only concerns the Jewish remnant and not the Christians. They argue that since the word "church" which refers to the body of Christ in the New Testament is not found in the Olivet Discourse and in Revelation 4-18, therefore the church (i.e., all church-age Christians in this present dispensation) are not present during the Tribulation. Instead, the only Christians that will be present during the Tribulation are tribulation saints (i.e., unbelievers who turn to Christ during the Tribulation period) and will form the basis of the church in the next "dispensation". John Walvoord, in his book *The Rapture Question*, writes that *"like all other passages on the Tribulation, there is no reference in this section of Matthew to the church."* (Walvoord, p. 45) In his view, while the term "elect" is found in Matthew 24:22, there is nothing to indicate that this word was referring to the church or present church-age Christians.

Concerning the Book of Revelation, he continues with the observation that the word "church" is not present in Revelation in chapters 4-18. John Walvoord writes: *"it is notable that in this extended portion of Scripture not one mention of the church, the body of Christ, is found."* (Walvoord, p. 46) Concerning the words "saints" and the "elect" which are found in the Book of Revelation, John Walvoord writes that the word "saints" do not necessarily mean the church in the present church-age: "*while there is frequent mention of "saints" in both heaven and on earth, this is obviously a general reference that could apply to believers in any dispensation.*" (Walvoord, p. 46) He then goes on to argue that the church is in full view in Revelation 19 where it is seen in heaven as the Bride of the Lamb, which is in contrast to the saints on earth – the tribulation saints.

Therefore, according to pre-tribulationists, since the word "church" is no longer present in Revelation 4-18 and because the Tribulation in the Old Testament is known as "Jacob's trouble" (Jeremiah 30:7) which only concerns the nation of Israel, therefore the church in the present church-age (which refers to the body of Christ) will not participate in the Tribulation. I make three observations here.

God can fulfill His promises to Israel with Christians still on earth – in fact, He has already fulfilled one of them in Amos 9:15

To be sure, there are indeed promises that the Lord gives to the nation of Israel in the Old Testament that will be fulfilled during the end times. Jeremiah 30, for example, concerns the restoration of Israel after the time of Jacob's trouble – a reference to the day of the Lord. Zechariah 12-14 also describes a future time when Jerusalem will come under attack and the Lord "*sets out to destroy all the nations that attack Jerusalem*" (Zechariah 12:9), while Zechariah 14 describes the future time when the Lord comes and reigns from Jerusalem as king over the entire earth (Zechariah 14:8-9)

However, there have also been promises in the Old Testament concerning the re-gathering of Israel back to their land that have been fulfilled with Christians still on earth. In the Book of Amos, the Lord declares:

"I will plant Israel in their own land, never again to be uprooted from the land I have given them." (Amos 9:15)

When one looks at world history, it is arguable that the promise to re-gather the Jews back to their own land has been fulfilled, although at tremendous cost to the Jews who suffered through the holocaust. In the crucial moment of sympathy for the Jews after the events of the holocaust, the United Nations on 29 November 1947 passed a resolution to partition the land into "an independent Arab State, an independent Jewish State, and the City of Jerusalem." In an extraordinary vote, this UN resolution was adopted by two-thirds majority with 33 votes in favor, 13 against and 10 abstentions. This led to immediate Jewish-Arab fighting in Palestine and the expulsion of Jews from Arab and Muslim countries back to Israel, where the Jews have stayed ever since to this present day. The modern-day Israel is now the only Jewish state in the world at the land that the Lord had given them, where Jerusalem (the Old City) is.

The point that I am making here is that God's promises to Israel, such as the one in Amos 9:15 concerning the regathering of Jews back to the land, had been fulfilled even when Christians of this present church-age (as dispensationalists term it) are still around. Why should there be any difficulty in fulfilling the promises to Israel in Jeremiah 30 and Zechariah 12-14 when Christians are still on earth? In other words, why must Christians be taken out of the world first before the Lord can fulfill the promises that he made to Israel? The Lord can certainly fulfill those promises to Israel while Christians are still on earth and He has done so, in the case of Amos 9:15.

The mere fact that certain promises in the Bible were made to Israel in the end times should not mean that Christians must be raptured out of the world before it takes place. The logical fallacy that the pre-tribulationists have is that since majority of Old Testament end-times prophecy relates to Israel, means that the church should not be around when it takes place. There is nothing in the Old Testament books in Jeremiah or Isaiah or Zechariah that suggests that the church would be removed prior to these promises being fulfilled in Israel.

The word "church" must be considered in the context of each individual book in the Bible

The second observation I would make here is that the word church must be considered within the context of each individual book in the Bible. What was the author's intention in using a particular word or phrase?

Whenever the word "church" is used in the Book of Revelation, it is always addressed to the church in a specific geographical area (i.e., a local church). For example, Jesus says that the message is directed to the "seven churches" – the church in Ephesus, Smyrna, Pergamum, Thyatira, Sardis, Philadelphia and Laodicea. Therefore, in Revelation 1-3, the word church has always been used to describe a particular church associated in a geographical area, which we now know refers to modern day Turkey. A closer examination of Revelation shows that the word "church" was never mentioned anywhere else from Chapter 4 to 21, except in Chapter 22 at the end of Revelation where the Lord Jesus himself says this:

*"I, Jesus, have sent my angel to give you this testimony for the **churches**. I am the Root and the Offspring of David, and the bright Morning Star."* (Revelation 22:16) (*emphasis added*)

It is quite clear from the plain and natural language of Revelation 22:16 that this entire testimony in the Book of Revelation was "for the churches" – and that therefore it should concern all the seven churches and by extension, the Christians. Dispensational pre-tribulationalists, however, point to the fact that since the word "church" is absent from Revelation 4-18, therefore the church must have been raptured to heaven. According to them, the saints and elect that are still on earth only refer to the tribulation saints.

I note that whenever Jesus uses the word "church" in Revelation, it is directed to a specific church associated with a geographical area, or the local church. At the end of Revelation, Jesus says that this message is given as a testimony to all the churches. Taken in context that he was addressing the seven churches at the beginning of Revelation, the word "churches" in Revelation 22:16 would mean all the seven churches that he had initially addressed the message to. In other words, the entire message of Revelation, from the beginning to the end in Revelation 22, would have been directed to the seven churches as a testimony to them.

This is an important point because, if this testimony on Revelation is given to the churches, then naturally it should concern the church – who are made up of present-day Christians. But apart from the local church, could the word "church" mean something else? I believe it does. Notice that in Revelation 2-3, the "church" that Jesus singles out represent an archetype of the church in different circumstances. In other words, the churches at that time period represent a type of church in the modern-day period.

Ephesus, for example, represents a church that has worked hard and persevered, and yet has forsaken the love they had for Christ at first. The church in Smyrna represents a church that has suffered afflictions and lives in poverty and will suffer persecution in the future. The church in Pergamum represents a church that remains faithful and true to Christ but allows false teachers in their midst to influence them. The church in Philadelphia represents a church that has little strength but has kept God's word to endure patiently and has not denied his name. Jesus gives the promise to the church in Philadelphia that *"since you have kept my command to endure patiently, I will also keep you from the hour of trial that is going to come on the whole world to test the inhabitants of the earth."* (Revelation 3:10) Pre-tribulationists love to quote Revelation 3:10 as evidence that the church will not go through the Tribulation. John Darby, for instance, claimed that all faithful Christians belong to the "Philadelphia" church and will be raptured before the Tribulation comes. We will come to this in the next chapter when we firmly deal with the arguments that pre-tribulationists use to support their view.

The point I am making is that whenever Jesus uses the word "church", it refers to either the local church (i.e., the church in

Ephesus, Smyrna, Thyatira, etc.) or to a type of church (i.e., the church in persecution, the lukewarm church, the church that looks alive from the outside but is in fact dead, etc.) Since virtually all the local churches mentioned in Revelation in ancient Turkey no longer exist, and since the book of Revelation was given to Christians to reveal what must take place in the future, it is reasonable to assume that the word "church" is now directed to a *type* of church in the present modern-day world.

The simple reason why the word "church" is not used in Revelation 4-18 is because when John is caught up to heaven to see what must take place in the future (Revelation 4:1-2), John does not see individual local churches or types of churches but rather all the saints and the elect – all the Christians around the world. And since the word "church" is always used to describe a church in a particular geographical area or as an *archetype* of the church, the words "saints" and "elect" are used instead which are proper terms to describe all Christians around the world.

To take an illustration, suppose you were instructed to write a letter to address a specific issue in the church in Princeton, South Carolina, and then asked to describe a scene where you see global events that affect all Christians around the world. How would you write this letter? You would write the letter addressed "To the church in Princeton, South Carolina", and follow this by describing global events that concern "the saints and elect" or concerning "the Christians". You wouldn't write a letter addressed to the church in Princeton, South Carolina and then describe global events that concern "the church" – because the next logical question after addressing the seven churches is – which "church" are you referring to?

I believe that the Lord Jesus, having initially addressed the letter to the seven churches, now turns to show John what will happen to all Christians around the world, and John uses the word saints and elect in the Revelation 4-18, in contrast to the word "church" which refers to a church in a specific geographical area or type of church, simply because he is now describing events that will happen to all Christians in the world. The word "saints" and "elect" in the New Testament are perfectly normal terms that describe born-again believers.

Notice that at the end of the Revelation in Chapter 22, Jesus himself says *"I have sent my angel to give you this testimony for the* **churches***."* (*emphasis added*) It would be rather strange to say then, that the first part of Revelation is addressed to the church but the second part after Chapter 3 to 18 is addressed to tribulation saints. Jesus clearly had the church in mind from start to finish – the logical conclusion is that the entire testimony was for the church.

The Lord Jesus gave us the Revelation to encourage us through tribulation

The character of the Lord Jesus is that he tells Christians what to expect in the future so that they can be prepared for it. Jesus never promised Christians relief from trouble but promises to take Christians through it. He says ***"In the world ye shall have tribulation: but be of good cheer; I have overcome the world."*** (John 16:33 KJV) (*emphasis added*)

There are several depictions of the sufferings that Christians will go through in Revelation. Many Christians will be martyred. The Apostle John writes in Revelation 13:10:

"If anyone is to go into captivity, into captivity they will go. If anyone is to be killed with the sword, with the sword they will be killed. **This calls for patient endurance and faithfulness on the part of God's people.**" (Revelation 13:10) (*emphasis added*)

The call for patient endurance and faithfulness is therefore given to God's people. Who then are God's people? Are they only the Jews, as pre-tribulationists put it? No, the Apostle Paul tells us in Romans 9:25-26:

"As he [the Lord] says in Hosea: "I will call them 'my people' who are not my people; and I will call her 'my loved one' who is not my loved one", and "In the very place where it was said to them, 'You are not my people,' there they will be called 'children of the living God.'" (Romans 9:25-26)

God's people clearly refer to both Jew and Gentile believers, and the call to endure is given to all Christians. And this command to endure is repeated in Revelation:

"This calls for patient endurance on the part of the **people of God** *who keep his commands and remain faithful to Jesus."* (Revelation 14:12) (*emphasis added*)

The themes of patient endurance and faithfulness are recurring themes that are repeated throughout Revelation. The reason why the call to endure and to be faithful is so urgent and important is that because many Christians will be martyred during the Great

Tribulation. John describes that the number of Christians that come out during the Great Tribulation as a great multitude that no one could count:

> "*After this I looked, and there before me was a **great multitude that no one could count, from every nation, tribe, people and language**, standing before the throne and before the Lamb. They were wearing white robes and were holding palm branches in their hands.*" (Revelation 7:9) (*emphasis added*)

And John continues:

> "*Then one of the elders asked me, "These in white robes – who are they, and where did they come from?" I answered, "Sir, you know." And he said, "**These are they who have come out of the Great Tribulation**; they have washed their robes and made them white in the blood of the Lamb.*" (Revelation 7:13) (*emphasis added*)

The elder tells John that these saints who have been martyred will be led to everlasting springs of water and God will wipe away every tear from their eyes. (Revelation 7:17) I would just pause here to make three important observations.

First, Christians will definitely be present during the Great Tribulation. These Christians will be from every nation, tribe, people and language. There will be a great multitude of Christians that will "come out of the Great Tribulation". Given the extremely large number from every nation, tribe, people and language, it is unlikely to refer to tribulation saints that have only recently started to put their faith in Christ. Had Jesus raptured the entire church before the Tribulation, it would take a stretch of imagination to imagine how so many Christians (a great multitude that no one can count) came out of the Great Tribulation. It is theoretically possible to evangelize a huge multitude of people during the Great Tribulation for them to become tribulation saints, but again, this is unlikely given the scale of the multitude that John describes. I believe that this multitude refers to all Christians who went through the Great Tribulation and were martyred for their faith.

Second, this great multitude in white robes cannot refer to those who have been raptured – because as the Apostle Paul points out in 1 Thessalonians 4:15-16, the rapture occurs for the entire church which includes those who have died or fallen asleep before the coming of Christ. Clearly, John was only referring to a specific group of people here – those who have **come out of the Great Tribulation** – and not those Christians who have fallen asleep before Christ had come (which would have also been an innumerable multitude).

Third, could this great multitude in white robes refer to tribulation saints who survive the Great Tribulation and go into the Millennial Kingdom? I do not think so – because John sees them "before the throne of God" (Revelation 7:15). They were given white robes just like those who had been martyred earlier on for their faith. Those who had been martyred earlier on *"were told to wait a little longer, until the full number of their fellow servants, their brothers and sisters, were killed just as they had been."* (Revelation 6:11) Clearly, a lot of Christians were still going to die in the Great Tribulation, and the great multitude in white robes probably represented those Christians.

I believe that the Lord Jesus gave Christians the Revelation to encourage them to endure and stay faithful, even to the point of death. Jesus says: "***Be faithful, even to the point of death***, *and I will give you life as your victor's crown.*" (Revelation 2:10) (*emphasis added*) Clearly, Jesus knew that many people were going to die during the Great Tribulation – but the comforting news is that martyrdom will only speed up the process of the saints going to heaven. And Jesus tells Christians to be faithful even to the point of death, and they will receive eternal life in Christ.

The pre-tribulationist position that Revelation 4-18 is not applicable to Christians of this present church age is certainly a precarious position. The book of Revelation is full of exhortations and words of encouragement to endure until the very end and it is difficult to imagine that Jesus would give Christians the Revelation but yet take them out of the Tribulation before it comes. Notice that the exhortation to be faithful even to the point of death is given to the churches – not to the tribulation saints as pre-tribulationists would have it. Why would Jesus give this encouragement to the churches if they are not going through the Tribulation? It would just make entire sections of Revelation 4-18 purely academic for Christians; it is of no practical use to them in the future.

At the beginning of Revelation, the Lord Jesus promises each of the seven churches that he will reward those who are "victorious" and "overcome" with eternal life. For example, Jesus says "*To the one who is victorious, I will give the right to eat from the tree of life, which is in the paradise of God*" (Revelation 2:7) and "*The one who is victorious will not be hurt at all by the second death.*"

(Revelation 2:11) These exhortations were clearly addressed to the church – or present-day church as dispensationalists like to put it. Notice that at the end of Revelation, when Jesus speaks of the new heaven and the new earth, he says: "*Those who are* **victorious** *will inherit all this, and I will be their God and they will be my children.*" (Revelation 21:7) (*emphasis added*) Jesus was clearly addressing one audience – the churches – and not a separate group of tribulation saints when he made this promise. I do not believe that the dispensational teaching that there will be two separate groups of Christians – the church before the Tribulation and the tribulation saints during the Tribulation – is a convincing distinction given that Jesus mentions the "victorious" ones at the beginning and at the end of the Book of Revelation. Jesus clearly only had in mind one audience when he made these promises and that was to the church.

Interestingly, it should be noted that the word "church" is neither found in Chapters 19, 20 and 21 of the Book of Revelation which concern the Millennial Kingdom and the Bride of the Lamb. Does one seriously conclude that these passages do not concern the present-day church at all because the word "church" is not present there? Certainly, these passages give a glimpse of the eternal reward that Christians would receive in the future – eternal life. Just because the word "church" is not present in these passages does not mean that the church is not the Bride of the Lamb. It is just illogical to argue that just because the word "church" is not in these passages it follows that the church is not there.

Finally, if pre-tribulationists are right that Chapters 4-18 of Revelation do not concern the present-day Christians but only tribulation saints, then it logically follows that Chapters 1-3 which contain all of Jesus' exhortations to the church to overcome and be victorious, would not be addressed to tribulation saints but only to the church. This position is completely untenable because the tribulation saints are precisely the kind of people who need to hear Jesus' words to overcome, endure and be victorious. Yet pre-tribulationists argue that Chapters 1-3 are only addressed to the church, and so Jesus' words of encouragement to endure and overcome will logically not be applicable to tribulation saints.

#6 The claim that God deals with Israel and the present-day church in separate dispensations or time periods is unbiblical

The dispensational teaching that God deals with Israel and the church in separate time periods – and that the church will be raptured before the Tribulation leaving only Israel and unbelievers to go through the Tribulation – is fundamentally unbiblical because it is not supported by any verse in scripture. It simply does not take into account the purpose of the church in relation to Israel's salvation, and vice versa. While the Bible does contain Old Testament promises concerning Israel in the end times, there is nothing to indicate that the church must be raptured first before God can fulfill His promises to Israel. When one studies the Old Testament prophets – Jeremiah, Isaiah, Zachariah and Ezekiel for example, there is not a single verse which says that only Israel and not the church, will be present on earth when God fulfills all the promises he made to Israel. As discussed in the previous chapter, God has in fact already fulfilled one promise he made to Israel concerning the regathering of Israel back to their native land in Amos 9:15 – all this happened while the church is still present on earth. The idea that the church is a New Testament entity that is distinct from Israel does not *ipso facto* mean that the church should not be present when God fulfills the promises to Israel in the end times.

In fact, God has fulfilled some of the judgments described in Leviticus 26:27-39 to the Jewish nation of Israel while Christians were still on earth. God says to the Jews that if they do not listen to God and remain hostile towards him, He will *"make their hearts so fearful in the lands of the enemies that the sound of a windblown leaf will put them to flight…those of you who are left will waste away in the lands of their enemies because of their sins; also because of their ancestors' sins they will waste away."* When one reads the horrors of the holocaust that happened to the scattered Jews in Europe, it is not difficult to identify these sufferings with the judgments prophesized in Leviticus 26. Since Israel has now be regathered back to their land (Amos 9:15), we can conclude that the Lord God will keep His promise never to uproot the Jews from the land again – Jews will be in their native land during the end times. But the point is that God is equally capable of blessing the nation of Israel and subjecting them to judgments even while the church is fully present on earth.

It should be noted that at the very root of dispensational teaching is John Nelson Darby's view that "the Jews" represented God's earthly people, while "the Church" represented God's "heavenly people". Darby thought that since Christians were already united with Christ, they have nothing else to wait for but Christ (i.e., there would be no intervening events that had to take place before the Lord would come for the church). By contrast, Darby thought that, since God still had to fulfill His promises to the Jewish nation of Israel, there would be a separate dispensation which concerns only Israel. This was based on Darby's understanding of Isaiah 32 when the *"Spirit would be poured out on the Jewish nation, and a king reign in righteousness."* In other words, Darby saw that the church would not participate in the particular program and promises that God had for Israel during the end times and Jesus would come for the church first, since the church was already united with Christ.

But the natural consequence of adopting Darby's view is that church is not involved at all in Israel's ultimate redemption at the last days. The Apostle Paul, however, does make it clear that the church serves a purpose in Israel's ultimate redemption in Romans 11.

Separately, there is a thorny problem on whether Jews who believe in Christ would be raptured before the Tribulation, or whether they would in fact participate in God's program for Israel during the Tribulation. In other words, are Jews who believe in Christ no longer part of Israel? Pre-tribulationists seem to think so.

John F. Walvoord in his book *The Rapture Question*, wrote that all Israelites (Jews) by natural birth will, upon receiving salvation through Jesus Christ, become part of the church (i.e., the body of Christ) and will therefore be cut off from the particular program and promises that God makes to Israel in the end times. In his view, believing Jews would no longer be part of "Israel" but rather the "body of Christ" and would be raptured before the Tribulation. However, the logical fallacy of this view is the implication is that "Israel" will always be composed of unbelieving Jews and never Jews who had received salvation in Jesus Christ. Based on John Walvoord's definition of "Israel", it logically follows that "Israel" will always be composed only of unbelieving Jews in this current dispensation and would therefore not be able to come to repentance, because they are always by definition composed of unbelieving Jews.

With respect, John Walvoord's views do not accord with Old Testament and New Testament teaching that before Christ returns to earth to establish his Millennial Kingdom, the nation of Israel must first be converted to Jesus as their Messiah. Jesus told the Jews in no uncertain terms: *"you will not see me again until you say, 'Blessed is he who comes in the name of the Lord.'"* (Matthew 23:39) Similarly in the Book of Acts, the Apostle Peter tells the Jews that they had *"disowned the Holy and Righteous One and asked that a murderer be released to you."* (Acts 3:14) Peter told the Jews to repent and turn to God, so that *"he may send the Messiah, who has been appointed for you – even Jesus."* (Acts 3:19-20) In the Book of Hosea, the Lord God says *"I will go and return to my place, till they acknowledge their offence, and seek my face: in their affliction they will seek me early."* (Hosea 5:15 KJV)

Arnold Fruchtenbaum in his work *The Footsteps of the Messiah: A Study of the Sequence of Prophetic Events (1982)* emphasizes that only when Israel confesses her sin and plead for the Messiah to return as one mourns for an only child and grieve bitterly for him as one grieves for a firstborn son, will Jesus return. (Zechariah 12:10-11) The Bible hints that in the end times, the nation of Israel in their suffering and affliction will look for Jesus: "*On the third day he will restore us, that we may live in his presence.*" (Hosea 6:1-2) As such, it is the clear teaching of scripture that before the Lord Jesus returns, Israel must first turn to Christ. It is therefore illogical to say that "Israel" solely comprises unbelieving Jews because the implication is that "Israel" can never repent if believing Jews are suddenly not part of "Israel" but now form the "church" or the "body of Christ".

There is nothing in scripture that suggests believing Jews would be raptured before the Tribulation and hence not be part of Israel in the end times; in fact, scripture tells us the very opposite that there will be 144,000 Jewish believers that will be sealed from "*all the tribes of Israel*" during the Tribulation (Revelation 7:4). Will pre-tribulationists seriously contend that these Jewish believers belong to the body of Christ and not Israel?

Furthermore, pre-tribulationists will have to deal with the question why the church is not at all involved with Israel's salvation during the Tribulation. In fact, the Apostle Paul himself in Romans 11 makes clear that the church does have a purpose in relation to Israel's ultimate salvation. He says:

> "*I do not want you to be ignorant of his mystery, my brothers and sisters, so that you may not be conceited: Israel has experienced a hardening in part until the full number of Gentiles has come in, and **in this way all Israel will be saved**. As it is written: "**The deliverer will come from Zion; he will turn godlessness away from Jacob**. And this is my covenant with them when I take away their sins.*"" (Romans 11:25-26) (*emphasis added*)

Notice that according to the Apostle Paul, the salvation of the church is tied to Israel and vice versa. He explains that the hardening of Israel's heart is only to bring in the full number of Gentile believers, and in this way all Israel will be saved. The whole purpose of bringing Gentile believers to Christ is not to prepare them to be raptured to heaven while leaving the Jewish nation behind; the whole purpose of evangelizing the Gentile church is to bring Israel to faith. God's program for Israel is never separated from the program that he has for the church – which is to bring all Jews and Gentiles as one flock to faith in Christ.

Therefore, the Old Testament promises to Israel should be read in context with God's plan to bring the Jewish nation of Israel to faith, which are never separated from God's divine purpose with the church on earth. The dispensational theory that Israel and the church are distinct and unique entities and that God deals with both separately in different time periods is an artificial distinction – God clearly uses the church to accomplish his mission with Israel and this would be no different during the end times when **all** Israel will be truly saved. Notice that the Apostle Paul says that when the church has reached its full number, **in this way** all Israel will be saved. Quite clearly, not all Israel has been saved yet during the Tribulation and the Apostle Paul is clear that the church has a purpose in bringing all Israel to salvation.

It is very interesting that the Apostle Paul then goes on to say that the hardening of Israel is to provoke them to jealously: "*but rather through their fall salvation is come unto the Gentiles, for to provoke them to **jealousy**.*" (Romans 11:11 KJV) (*emphasis added*) There is a substantial difference between the word "jealousy" and "envy" – jealousy is used when you are unhappy and angry that someone has something that *belongs* to you. This is why the Lord God told the people of Israel: *"For thou shalt worship no other god: for the Lord, whose name is Jealous, is a jealous God."* (Exodus 34:14 KJV) In other words, worship belongs to God and to God alone because Israel is His first-born son (Exodus 4:22 KJV) – Israel's worship rightfully belongs to Him. The word "envy", however, is a feeling of desire and want for something that someone has that does *not* belong to you – covetousness is closely associated with envy because it is the desire for something that does not rightfully belong to you.

Paul uses the word "jealousy" to connote an important point that salvation rightfully belongs to the Jews. Christianity is in fact derived from Jewish roots – it belongs to the Jews. The purpose of evangelizing the Gentile church is to provoke Israel to jealousy to faith in Jesus Christ – which is rightfully theirs. Gentiles are therefore grafted into the Jewish faith. Paul then warns the Gentiles: *"Do not consider yourself to be superior to those other branches…**you do not support the root, but the root supports you.**"* (Romans 11:18) (*emphasis added*) Therefore the faith that Gentiles have in Christ belongs to Jewish roots. This raises some important questions. If Christians belong to Jewish roots, why should the Gentile church and all believers be given the privilege of being raptured before the Tribulation and before all Israel and the Jews are brought to salvation in Christ? How would the nation of Israel be provoked to jealousy if the church was raptured out of the world before the Tribulation? Notice that the Apostle Paul tells the Gentile Christians not to consider themselves superior to the unbelieving Jews – those natural branches that had been cut off due to unbelief. Paul says: *"And if they do not persist in unbelief, they will be grafted in, for*

God is able to graft them in again…how much more readily will these, the natural branches, be grafted into their own olive tree!" (Romans 11:23-24) In other words, Gentile Christians should not consider themselves superior or more privileged than unbelieving Jews, for God is able to graft them back into the root – that is, faith in Jesus Christ. Neither should the Gentile church expect that they would be raptured out of the world before Israel and the Jews are brought to salvation, for the Gentile church is grafted into the Jewish faith with Jewish roots. Christians are not superior to unbelieving Jews or entitled to privileged treatment as far as the gospel is concerned. Paul says: *"Do not be arrogant, but tremble. For if God did not spare the natural branches, he will not spare you either."* (Romans 11:20-21) Paul's teaching is therefore antithetical to Darby's dispensational view that the church represented God's "heavenly people", while Jews represented God's "earthly people", and that Christ would come for the church first. God is still very much jealous for unsaved Jews as He is for the church: *"Thus saith the Lord of hosts; I am jealous for Jerusalem and for Zion with a great jealousy."* (Zechariah 1:14-15 KJV)

The simple truth is that God's purposes for the church and for Israel have always been intertwined with each other. Notice that Israel has experienced a hardening so that the full number of Gentile believers will be brought in. So even though Israel and the church are theoretically separate, the hardening of Israel causes the church to increase in number! And likewise, once the church has reached its full number, then in this way all Israel will be saved. Both Israel and the church have always been inextricably linked in God's purpose for salvation and redemption of his people. Darby's view that both the church and Israel are distinctly separate, and that God will deal with each of them separately in different dispensations is neither supported by scripture nor in line with the gospel – it is unbiblical. Romans 11 is a simple lesson on how both the church and Israel's salvation are inextricably linked, and the Apostle Paul makes it clear that all Israel will be saved through the full number of Gentile believers coming to faith. Clearly, the Apostle Paul hints that there will be a role for the church to play in Israel's ultimate salvation during the end times when all Israel will be saved.

I do not believe that there will be a pre-tribulation rapture where Christians and believing Jews will be caught up, leaving behind only the unbelieving Jewish remnant which God solely deals with. The Bible teaches that while God has His promises to Israel in the end times, the purpose of the church and Israel's salvation are inextricably tied and linked together. God will use the church to bring all Israel to faith. Salvation in Christ rightfully belongs to the Jews; Gentiles were grafted in by faith. The dispensational theory that the church should be taken out before God deals with Israel and that both have separate purposes in God's divine plan is an artificial distinction that ignores the true purpose that God has for the church in Israel's redemption, and vice versa.

#7 The practical consequence of preaching a secret rapture is to ill-equip the church for future tribulation and persecution

The practical consequences of preaching a secret pre-tribulational rapture to Christians is in reality to ill-equip the church for future trials and tribulations, albeit on a local scale in this present time.

This is now a major problem because, since John Nelson Darby and C. I. Scofield, there has been a widespread teaching in America, particularly among evangelicals, that before the big trouble Christ would come and take the church and all believers out of the world. Subsequently, missionaries from America have, while spreading the gospel around the world, also carried this idea that Christians will be raptured to heaven before the Tribulation comes.

Ruth B. Graham (the wife of Evangelist Billy Graham) in a letter dated March 31, 1975 addressed to David MacPherson who authored the book *"Late Great Pre-Trib Rapture"*, wrote of her personal experience in China where persecution and tribulation had already started for Chinese Christians. She wrote, from her personal experience of Christians suffering around the world, that this should make pre-tribulationists do some serious thinking about whether the message of a pre-tribulation rapture benefits the church at all. While the tribulation that Christians in some parts of China are going through are certainly nothing compared to the Great Tribulation, Ruth made an astute observation that *"there is only so much one can suffer"* to the point of death.

Ruth wrote that she would rather prepare herself to go through the Tribulation and have the pleasant surprise of being raptured before the Tribulation, than to be caught by surprise when the real Tribulation comes and not being raptured. Ruth recounts how she spoke to a missionary from China who told her that one of her biggest regrets was *"not having prepared the Chinese Christians for the tribulation they would undergo"*, but instead preaching that before the big trouble comes Jesus would come for them first. The experiences of missionaries on the ground in places where Christians are experiencing real tribulation is reason to give pause and re-think the pre-tribulation rapture.

When one reads about the tribulation that Christians in China are suffering today, the words of the Lord Jesus in the Book of Revelation to the church in Smyrna which suffered great persecution comes to mind: *"Be faithful, even to the point of death, and I will give you life as your victor's crown."* (Revelation 2:10) Jesus did not say, "be faithful and I will rapture you". He said be faithful even to the point of death, and you will receive everlasting life as a reward.

Corrie ten Boom, who herself went through the holocaust and the Nazi concentration camps and who was instrumental in helping many Jewish people escape from the Nazis, wrote in a 1974 letter from China to America's pastors concerning the Tribulation that there are some teachers in America that teach that there will be no Tribulation and Christians will be able to escape from the big trouble. She wrote that these are *"some of the false teachers that Jesus was warning us to expect in the latter days"* whom have very little knowledge of the actual persecution that was going around the world and in countries where Christians were being put to death for their faith in Jesus Christ.

Corrie recounts that in China, the Christians were told *"Don't worry, before the tribulation comes you will be raptured"* by American missionaries. Then came a terrible persecution. Many Chinese Christians were thrown in prison and tortured to death for their faith. Later she heard a Bishop from China say sadly, *"We have failed. We should have made the people strong for persecution rather than telling them Jesus would come first."*

Corrie said that this experience made her think seriously about the pre-tribulation rapture view and that she should instead be teaching people how to stand strong when tribulation comes – to "*stand and not faint*", rather than teach that before the Tribulation Jesus would come and rapture them to heaven.

Corrie recounts that while she was in a nation in Africa, a new government had just come to power and started persecuting Christians. The Christians in her district were told to go to the police station and register. When they went to the police station, they were arrested and then executed. This continued for the next day, and the next. She wrote that all the Christians in her district were systematically being murdered. During that time, Corrie spoke at a little church in that African district where the congregation was filled with fear and tension that they were next in line to be killed. She then told the church a story about her childhood of how her father would give her just enough money for her journey right before she boarded the train to Amsterdam. She told the African congregation: "*Our Father in Heaven knows when you will need the strength to be a martyr for Jesus Christ. He will supply you all you need just in time.*" Suddenly a spirit of joy descended on the church and people started to sing to the Lord. Later that week, half the congregation in the church was executed; and sometime later she heard that the other half was also martyred. But Corrie remembered the words of the Lord Jesus that to "*all those who remained faithful to the end, He would give a crown of life.*"

The point that Corrie was making in her letter is that the church must not wait till the Tribulation comes before Christians start preparing. Christians need to start preparing for the Tribulation now, and this involves a change in mindset and attitude towards the way we view the rapture. This attitude was born out of Corrie ten Boom's personal experience with Christians suffering the persecution. As Ruth Graham and Corrie notes, persecution and tribulation had already come for some members of the body of Christ living in China and Africa. While this was not the "Great Tribulation", there is only so much suffering that one can endure to the point of death.

The danger of preaching a pre-tribulation rapture is to ill-equip the church for the actual persecution and tribulation that will come in the future, even on a local scale (as Ruth points out in China). Christians that think they will not go through the Great Tribulation will be surprised and completely caught off guard when real tribulation comes – even on a local scale. The experience of Corrie ten Boom and Ruth Graham in China should be a sobering reminder of the consequence of preaching a pre-tribulational rapture to the church, especially in countries experiencing persecution. It does nothing to equip the church for tribulation and the "fiery trial" that comes to test them (1 Peter 4:12)

As we have seen from the scriptures in the earlier chapters, we see that the Lord Jesus is constantly telling Christians to be strong, to endure and to overcome tribulation. This is a recurring theme throughout the New Testament. In fact, the Lord Jesus never promised to take Christians out of trouble. Jesus said: *"These things I have spoken unto you, that in me ye might have peace.* ***In the world ye shall have tribulation****: but be of good cheer; I have overcome the world."* (John 16:33 KJV) (*emphasis added*) Before he was crucified, he prayed concerning his disciples:

"My prayer is not that you take them out of the world but that you protect them from the evil one." (John 17:15)

In the book of Revelation, Jesus tells the Christians in each of the seven churches to hold fast in the faith and endure so that they may be "victorious". To the church in Smyrna, Jesus said: *"Do not be afraid of what you are about to suffer. I tell you, the devil will put some of you in prison to test you, and you will suffer persecution for ten days. **Be faithful, even to the point of death**, and I will give you life as your victor's crown."* (Revelation 2:10) (*emphasis added*) Clearly, the early church was already experiencing tribulation and the command that Jesus gives is for them to be faithful to the point of death.

The Bible is full of exhortations from the Lord Jesus to prepare Christians for the coming Tribulation and persecution. The Great Tribulation will be on a scale like no other, with widespread universal persecution of all Christians around the world: *"ye shall be hated of all nations for my name's sake."* (Matthew 24:9 KJV) The tragedy is that the pre-tribulation rapture view has now turned Christians away from the necessity of preparing for tribulation and suffering, and instead having them focus on the imminency of Christ's return for them. This is exactly the kind of teaching that the Apostle Paul warned about in his second letter to the Thessalonians. And the effect this has had on the church is that Christians are now unprepared for tribulation. If Christians believe this teaching and are not raptured and go through the Tribulation, the day of the Lord will indeed catch them by surprise when it comes, and as Jesus predicted, many will turn away from the faith during the Tribulation (Matthew 24:10). Jesus promised Christians big trouble, and we should get ready for it when it comes.

Chapter 4

Debunking Common Pre-Tribulation Rapture Arguments

In this chapter, we will deal with the common arguments that pre-tribulationists use to justify that there will be a rapture before the Tribulation. Pre-tribulationists view that the church and Israel are unique and distinct entities that God deals with separately in the end times, and Jesus will rapture the church (i.e., his Bride) before he deals with Israel and unbelievers on earth during the Tribulation. As we examined the scriptures in the previous chapter, the logical conclusion from all the exhortations to endure, persevere and to be faithful to the point of death, would not make much sense if Christians were to be taken out of the world before the big trouble happens.

Pre-tribulationists also claim that to reject the notion of Christ's imminent coming is to therefore abandon the hope of his imminent return. Having searched the scriptures, we can see that expectation of Jesus' imminent return was exactly the root cause of the same fear that the Thessalonians had – that those who had already died had somehow 'missed out' on the Second Coming of Christ and had no hope of seeing Christ. It is rather telling that Paul tells the church in Thessalonica that Christ died for us so that, whether we are awake or asleep in death, we will live in Christ. Therefore, he says, encourage each other with these words. The true purpose of Paul telling Christians to encourage one another is not because they would be spared from the rapture, but rather even if they had 'missed' the Second Coming and had fallen asleep, they would still live in Christ and will be the first to be raised when Jesus comes: *the dead in Christ will rise first.*" (1 Thessalonians 4:16)

#1 Christians are not appointed to suffer wrath

Pre-tribulationists quote 1 Thessalonians 1:10 and 1 Thessalonians 5:9 as the basis that Christians are not appointed to suffer wrath and will be rescued from the coming wrath. They claim that before the start of the Tribulation, Jesus would come to take them to the Father's house in heaven (John 14:1-3). Furthermore, in Revelation 3:10, Jesus promises the church in Philadelphia that he will "keep them from the hour of trial that is going to come on the whole world to test the inhabitants of the earth." They argue that the totality of scripture points towards a pre-tribulation rapture where Christians will be spared from God's wrath during the Tribulation.

John Walvoord, in his book *The Rapture Question*, wrote that the rapture of the saints is the comforting hope that the

Apostle Paul was referring to in his letter to the Thessalonians. He writes that the exhortation to encourage each other found in 1 Thessalonians 4:13-18 is because *"the church is promised the comfort of translation…which is regarded as an imminent event."* (Walvoord, p. 35) In his view, the reason why the Apostle Paul tells the church in Thessalonica to comfort each other with these words is because they would be raptured before the Tribulation comes. However, a closer examination of scripture will reveal that the reason why Paul tells the church in Thessalonica to *encourage each other with these words* is due to a different reason altogether.

I will first deal with the point that the Apostle Paul's exhortation to *encourage each other with these words* implies that the church is promised comfort from the Tribulation through the rapture, followed by the second point that the church is not appointed to suffer wrath.

Concerning the first point that Paul's exhortation to *encourage each other with these words* implies that Christians will be taken out of the Tribulation, the error that John Walvoord and other pre-tribulationists have is taking verses out of context. It is necessary to first ask the question – why did the Apostle Paul write to the Thessalonians? What was the evil he was trying to address when he spoke about the rapture?

In Chapter 3 of this book, we discussed that the prevalent Greek thinking at that time in Ancient Greece was that death was the end of all things. Those who had died had no hope and would sleep in an eternal slumber. The Greeks thought that there was no resurrection of the dead. Clearly, this Greek thinking was starting to seep into the church in Thessalonica where some members of the church had already died before the coming of Christ. The church thought that those who had died had 'missed' the Second Coming of Christ and would therefore miss out on the resurrection.

This is why the Apostle Paul in 1 Thessalonians 4:13 writes: *"Brothers and sisters, we do not want you to be uninformed about those who sleep in death, so that you do not grieve like the rest of mankind, who have no hope."* Clearly, Paul was addressing the misconception that those who had died would not be participating in the resurrection or the Second Coming, and he was correcting the Thessalonians' apparent lack of knowledge about the resurrection and the Second Coming. Paul also mentions the *"rest of mankind, who have no hope"*, which reflects the prevalent Greek thinking that once a man died, there was no hope and no resurrection for him. This Greek thinking had clearly seeped into the church, and the context of Paul's message was to clearly address this idea that death is the end for a believer.

Notice that when the Apostle Paul tells the church in Thessalonica to encourage each other with these words, Paul is always writing in the context of believers in the church who have died and were thought to have 'missed' the Second Coming. So in 1 Thessalonians 3:14-18, the Apostle Paul writes:

*"For we believe that Jesus died and rose again, and so we believe that **God will bring with Jesus those who have fallen asleep in him.** According to the Lord's word, we tell you that we who are still alive, who are left until the coming of the Lord, **will certainly not precede those who have fallen asleep**. For the Lord himself will come down*

*from heaven, with a loud command, with the voice of the archangel and with the trumpet call of God, **and the dead in Christ will rise first**. After that, we who are still alive and are left will be caught up together with them in the clouds to meet the Lord in the air. And so we will be with the Lord forever. **Therefore encourage one another with these words**.*" (*emphasis added*)

It is quite clear that Paul puts an emphasis on those who have died in Christ. He says to the church that those who have died in Christ would not miss out on the resurrection – Paul is clear that those who are left when the Lord Jesus comes will certainly not precede those who have fallen asleep: the dead in Christ will rise first. And Paul says, therefore encourage each other with these words. The context in which Paul wrote this letter to the Thessalonians was to clearly ease their minds about those who had fallen asleep and the idea that they had "missed" the resurrection and the Second Coming. Subsequently in 1 Thessalonians 5:8-11, Paul writes:

*"But since we belong to the day, let us be sober, putting on faith and love as a breastplate, and the hope of salvation as a helmet. For God did not appoint us to suffer wrath but to receive salvation through our Lord Jesus Christ. **He died for us so that, whether we are awake or asleep, we may live together with him**. Therefore **encourage one another** and build each other up, just as in fact you are doing.*" (*emphasis added*)

Again, just before Paul tells the church to encourage each other in verse 11, Paul reiterates the point that Jesus died for Christians so that, whether we are awake or asleep, we may live together with him (verse 10). In other words, the context in which Paul wrote these words of encouragement is precisely to encourage the Thessalonians that those who had already died will still be living in Christ. Therefore, it does not matter if the Christian is dead or alive – because in Christ, we will live together with him. It is in this context that Paul tells the church to encourage each other and to correct the Greek thinking that the dead have no hope or no resurrection.

Pre-tribulationists have mistakenly characterized Paul's exhortation to encourage one another as the basis that the church would be raptured before the Tribulation. Paul clearly was not referring to the Tribulation when he wrote to the Thessalonians. He was addressing the thinking that the dead had no hope, and Paul tells them that all Christians – whether awake or asleep – will live together with Christ. It is in this context that Paul is writing to the Thessalonians and the rapture passages should be interpreted as such.

Second, pre-tribulationists point to the scripture verses which state that Christians are not appointed to suffer wrath but are rescued from the coming wrath (1 Thessalonians 1:10) as the basis for Christians being raptured to heaven before the start of the Tribulation. And since God pours out his wrath on mankind during the Tribulation, they claim that it logically follows that Christians will not suffer wrath but will be raptured to heaven before the Tribulation occurs.

Let's take a closer look at what the Apostle Paul wrote to the church in Thessalonica. Paul writes to the church in Thessalonica:

"And to wait for his Son from heaven, whom he raised from the dead, even Jesus, which delivered us from the wrath to come." (1 Thessalonians 1:8 KJV)

Pre-tribulationists point to the fact that since the promise to be delivered from wrath is the past tense, therefore Christians would already have been saved from the wrath that is to come and would be raptured before the Tribulation comes, since the Tribulation is a manifestation of God's wrath. However, could the Apostle Paul mean something else when he mentioned the word "wrath"? Did the Lord Jesus die for us so that we can be spared from the Great Tribulation, or from hell – the lake of fire – which is the ultimate expression of God's wrath?

Again, when one examines the scripture verses in more detail, we can see that the "wrath" that the Apostle Paul was referring to is tied to the salvation from believing in Jesus and the prevalent Greek thinking that there was no hope for the dead, which Paul was trying to address in his letter to the Thessalonians. Therefore in 1 Thessalonians 5:9, Paul writes: "For God did not appoint us to suffer wrath but ***to receive salvation through our Lord Jesus Christ.***" (*emphasis added*) The only logical implication from this statement is that those who do not receive salvation through the Lord Jesus *will* suffer wrath. Why will they suffer wrath? What kind of wrath will they suffer? The Apostle John provides an answer:

"For God did not send his Son into the world to condemn the world, but to save the world through him. Whoever believes in him is not condemned, but whoever does not believe stands condemned already because they have not believed in the name of God's one and only Son." (John 3:17-18)

Clearly, the "wrath" that the Apostle Paul was referring to was not the Great Tribulation because, the one who rejects Christ and does not have salvation will not be appointed to go through the "Great Tribulation", rather he will suffer the true wrath of God which is the eternal consignment to hell – or the lake of fire – where they will be tormented day and night for eternity. In other words, the "Great Tribulation" pales in comparison to the coming wrath reserved for unbelievers and those who reject the salvation from Christ. It is in this context of salvation in Jesus Christ that we truly understand what the Apostle Paul meant that Christians are not appointed to suffer wrath and that Jesus saved us from the coming wrath – that is – the righteous judgment of God on unbelievers.

Finally, it is necessary to state the obvious that the Tribulation only lasts 7 years while eternal wrath will last forever. Those who do not believe in Christ are not appointed to suffer the Tribulation – they are appointed for something worse – that is hell, the lake of fire – and this is the eternal wrath of God that one suffers for rejecting the salvation from Jesus Christ. The real wrath that Christians are rescued from is eternal wrath, not the 7 years of Tribulation. Therefore Paul emphasizes the salvation we have in Jesus Christ immediately after stating that Christians are not appointed to suffer wrath in 1 Thessalonians 5:9. The salvation that we have in Jesus Christ is meant to rescue Christians from eternal wrath – not the 7 year Tribulation period.

#2 The word "church" disappears from Revelation 4-18 because the church has raptured into heaven

Pre-tribulationists argue that since the word *ekklesia* or "church" is not present in Revelation 4-18, therefore the "church" would have already been raptured to heaven during the Tribulation. This is a rather precarious argument. John Walvoord writes in his book *The Rapture Question* that there is not a single mention of the local church in Chapters 4-18 of Revelation. Neither, he says, is there any single reference to the church in name or by any other peculiar title – such as the body of Christ – throughout the Book of Revelation. John then concedes that while there is a frequent mention of the word "saints" in heaven and on earth during the Tribulation, he says *"this is obviously a general reference that could apply to believers in any dispensation."* (Walvoord, p. 46) He writes that since the *"church is in view in the figure of the marriage"* in Revelation 19 as the Bride of the Lamb, this should be clearly contrasted with tribulation saints who are still on earth.

Therefore, according to John Walvoord, since the word church or the body of Christ is not mentioned in Chapters 4-18 of the Book of Revelation, the church itself is not present during the Tribulation because it has already been raptured to heaven. Furthermore, he argues, that while there is a frequent mention of "saints" in heaven and on earth, this could refer to believers in any dispensation (i.e., the word saints only refers to believers in this present church-age and not to tribulation saints, who are in a different dispensation at the end times).

It is quite easy to spot the logical fallacy in John Walvoord's argument. Using his own argument, it could be said that even if the word "church" is used in Chapters 4-18 of the Book of Revelation, the "church" may just refer to the body of Christ in that dispensation and excludes all church-age Christians in this present dispensation. It can also be argued that the word "saints" and "elect" are perfectly normal terms used to describe born-again believers, and as John Walvoord concedes, could refer to believers in any dispensation, which includes the believers in this present dispensation. John then goes on to say that the *"church is in view in the figure of marriage in Revelation 19"*, yet notice that the word "church" does not actually appear in Revelation 19, 20 or even 21 when Jesus describes the "new heaven and new earth". So if we were to use the "church" argument that dispensationalists deploy, we can equally say that the church is not included in Revelation 19 as the Bride of the Lamb because the word "church" is not there.

Similarly, the word "church" is not found in many books of the New Testament including Mark, Luke, John, 2 Timothy, Titus, 1 Peter, 2 Peter, 1 John, 2 John and Jude. Does this mean that these books in the Bible do not concern the church? It is simply untenable to say that just because the word "church" is not found in a particular section of scripture, therefore it does not apply to the church or that the church is not participating in the Tribulation. The word "Jesus" or "Messiah" is not used in the Hebrew text in Isaiah 53 (in reality the song about the suffering servant begins from Isaiah 52:13 but has been cut out from the chapter), but this does not mean that Isaiah 53 does not concern our Lord Jesus.

Furthermore, the word "church" is not found in any of the rapture passages in 1 Thessalonians 4. Could we then argue that the rapture would not involve the church, just because the word "church" is not there?

However, taking the dispensational view aside, could there be another reason why the word "church" is not found in Revelation 4-18? Notice that whenever the word "church' is used in the Book of Revelation, it is always addressed to a specific church in a geographical area. Jesus spoke to the seven churches in Asia which are Ephesus, Smyrna, Pergamum, Thyatira, Sardis, Philadelphia and Laodicea. These are the local churches associated with a geographical area. They can also refer to a *type* of church, so for example, the church in Smyrna and Philadelphia are an archetype of churches that are experiencing persecution and have little strength, while the church in Laodicea is an archetype of a lukewarm church, etc.

John Walvoord argues that the message to the seven churches in Asia is *"obviously contemporary to the first century"* (Walvoord, p. 46) and do not concern the church in the future. I disagree. I believe that the Lord Jesus gave the Book of Revelation not only to encourage these churches in Asia regarding specific issues that they were experiencing, but also for the wider church in the future. It is notable that even dispensationalists such as John Darby thought that present church-age Christians belong to the church in Philadelphia – the *"we are Philadelphia"* argument – and therefore Christians would be spared from the Tribulation. Notice that Jesus' promise to the church in Philadelphia: *"Since you have kept my command to endure patiently, I will also keep you from the hour of trial that is going to come on the whole world to test the inhabitants of the earth."* (Revelation 3:10) could have been interpreted to have been fulfilled during the great persecution of Christians under Emperor Nero in 64 A.D. after the great fire of Rome, but it clearly also affects the church at the future time when the hour of trial comes on the whole world to *"test the inhabitants of the earth"*. After all, the Book of Revelation was given to John to show the servants of Jesus Christ what will take place in the future (Revelation 1:1) and during the Tribulation.

The logical fallacy of the pre-tribulationist's argument is that because Revelation 1-3 only concerns the churches and contains messages that are obviously contemporary to the first century, therefore, it follows that Revelation 1-3 do not concern tribulation saints. Yet notice that Revelation 1-3 are the very verses that tribulation saints need to hear to have the courage to go through the Tribulation – the encouragement to endure patiently to the point of death, the promises of rewards to those who are "victorious". It is very unlikely that the first three chapters including the exhortation to endure to the point of death and rewards for perseverance and being victorious, are then suddenly not applicable to tribulation saints in Revelation 4-18 as they are meant for the church which has already been raptured. It becomes apparent that the Lord Jesus' command to the church in Revelation 1-3 to endure and be victorious would not make any sense if the church was raptured, leaving behind those tribulation saints who have no promises whatsoever for being victorious through the Tribulation as Chapters 1-3 were not directed to them. On the contrary, it makes logical sense for Jesus to give exhortations to the church to endure and be faithful to the point of death and to be victorious in Chapters 1-3, before telling them what must take place in the Tribulation in Chapters 4-18. Notice that at the end of the Book of Revelation, the Lord Jesus says that this testimony is addressed to the "churches".

I believe that the Apostle John, having just wrote to the seven local churches in Asia, did not use the word "church" while he was describing what would happen on earth for the simple reason that it concerned all Christians around the world. Since the word "church" is always used in conjunction with a local church or archetype of church in the Book of Revelation, the simple reason why the word "church" in Revelation 4-18 was not used is because it concerns all Christians around the world, and not a specific church or type of church. John, however, does use the word "saints, "elect" and "God's people", which are perfectly normal terms to describe born-again believers.

Who then are "God's people"? It is interesting that the Lord God Himself in the Old Testament, speaking in future terms, said through the prophet Hosea: "*I will say to those called 'Not my people,' 'You are my people'; and they will say, 'You are my God.'*" Clearly, the Lord was speaking of a future time when He will call those who are not His people, His people. These people clearly refer to all Christians in the future tense – whether Jew or Gentile.

Therefore, when John wrote in the Book of Revelation: "*This calls for patient endurance and faithfulness on the part of God's people*" in Revelation 13:10 and Revelation 14:12, he was clearly referring to all the Christians, not just Israel or the tribulation saints.

John Walvoord concedes that the words "elect" and "saints" could refer to Christians in any dispensation – but insists that church-age Christians are a separate group from tribulation saints. I do not think that there is a separate dispensation that will apply to Christians in the end times at all. There should only be two dispensations divided between the Old Testament and the New Testament. Notice that the Lord Jesus hints that there will only be two separate dispensations – those in the Old Covenant and the New Covenant. He says: "*And no man putteth new wine into old bottles; else the new wine will burst the bottles, and be spilled, and the bottles shall perish. But new wine must be put into new bottles; and both are preserved.*" (Luke 5:37 KJV) It is quite interesting that the Lord Jesus said that "*both are preserved*", implying that the promises and covenants in the Old Testament to Israel will also be preserved in the New Testament period under the New Covenant.

It is quite telling that at the end of the Revelation, the Lord Jesus says: "*I, Jesus, have sent my angel to give you this testimony for the **churches**.*" (Revelation 22:16) (*emphasis added*) which clearly implies that this entire testimony in Revelation is for the seven churches and by extension, to all Christians. Jesus clearly had in mind the church from start to finish and he clearly states that this testimony is for the churches. Concerning the "new heaven and new earth", the Lord Jesus promises that "*those who are victorious will inherit all this*" (Revelation 21:7), which is a clear reference to his exhortation to the seven churches to be victorious in Revelation 2-3.

The logical conclusion is that the entire Book of Revelation is addressed to the churches and by extension, to all Christians. The notion that there is a separate dispensation between present church-age Christians and future tribulation saints is artificial and renders large portions of the Book of Revelation, namely chapters 4-18, purely academic for present church-age Christians. I do not believe that the Lord Jesus would give us such large portions of information and detail about the end times to satisfy our curiosity. They are clearly given to prepare Christians for the Great Tribulation ahead. When one studies the character of the Lord Jesus in the synoptic gospels and the Book of John, we know that the Lord Jesus tells Christians ahead of time what must take place to prepare them for it, not to satisfy the curiosity of the reader. The Lord Jesus is a practical man. The future warnings and exhortations set out in Revelation are meant for practical application, not to satisfy one's curiosity about the end times.

#3 The promise in Revelation 3:10 to "keep you" from the hour of trial

Pre-tribulation scholars love to quote Revelation 3:10 as the basis for the church being raptured into heaven before the Tribulation comes. The Apostle John writes as follows:

> *"Because thou hast kept the word of my patience, I also will **keep thee from** the hour of temptation, which shall come upon all the world, to try them that dwell upon the earth."* (Revelation 3:10 KJV) (*emphasis added*)

Pre-tribulationists point to the fact that the church will be "kept" from the hour of trial or temptation as evidence that the church will be raptured to heaven before the Tribulation comes. John Nelson Darby thought that all Christians who patiently endure would be part of the "Philadelphia" church that would be raptured before the Tribulation – he wrote concerning the present church-age Christians that *"we are all Philadelphia"*.

The pre-tribulationist argument that the church would be kept from the hour of trial and therefore raptured before the Tribulation comes can be readily disposed of when we look at the intention of the Apostle John when he uses the word "*keep from*". Notice that when the Apostle John uses the word "keep from" in the Gospel of John, it means to be protected from something rather than to be taken out of the world. So for example, John records that Jesus prayed:

> "*I pray not that thou shouldest take them out of the world, but that thou shouldest **keep** them from the evil.*" (John 17:15 KJV)

The Greek word for "keep from" used in Revelation 3:10 tēresō is derived from the same Greek word "keep from" used in John 17:15 tērēsēs which means, in the context of John 17:15 to be kept and protected from evil. John uses the same variant of the word "keep" in Revelation 3:10 to bring home the exact same point that Jesus protects Christians from the evil one.

I believe that Revelation 3:10 should be read together with Jesus' prayer and desire expressed in John 17:15 that Christians should not be taken out of the world, but rather they would be kept from temptation and from the evil one. After all, it was Jesus who prayed that Christians should not be taken out of the world – why would he change his mind when he gave John the Revelation? No, I believe Jesus clearly meant in Revelation 3:10 that he would protect the church from evil because they had obeyed the command to endure patiently, not take them out of the world.

Notice also that the promise to "*keep thee from the hour of temptation*" is directly contingent on the church in Philadelphia keeping the Lord's command to endure patiently. And the church in Philadelphia, like the church in Smyrna, were experiencing persecution by the "synagogue of Satan". Therefore, the promise to be kept from the hour of trial does not mean the church would be taken out of from the world, but rather, it is because the church has already been enduring and suffering persecution that they are protected from the Great Tribulation.

The problem with the pre-tribulationist argument that all Christians belong to the church in "Philadelphia" should also be examined. Notice that this promise was given to only one out of the seven churches – it was not given to the church in Smyrna, which was also faithful and suffering persecution. Logically, there would be Christians in other churches that are faithful such as Smyrna, so why are they not promised the rapture? When happens to the other Christians in the other six churches?

Clearly, the promise to be kept from the hour of trial in Revelation 3:10 was only specific to the church in Philadelphia – the faithful church with little strength left. It was not given to the other six churches.

However, could the Lord Jesus have meant something else when he said *"I will keep thee from the hour of temptation?"* When one considers how Jesus may keep his church from the seven bowls of wrath poured out on the world during the Tribulation, the picture of Israel during the Plagues of Egypt comes to mind. The Lord God told Moses and Aaron: *"I will make a distinction between my people and your people."* (Exodus 8:23) In other words, while the Egyptians were suffering from the effects of the plagues, Israel was kept safe and protected from them. The Lord God kept the Israelites safe from the plagues without having to take them out of Egypt – they were spared from God's wrath without having to be "raptured" into heaven.

In the Book of Revelation, we find a similar reference to the woman who will give birth to a son, a male child, who will *"rule the nations with an iron scepter"* – clearly referring to Jesus. The Apostle John tells us that the *"woman fled into the wilderness to a place prepared for her by God, where she might be taken of for 1260 days"*. (Revelation 12:6) There has been considerable debate whether this woman refers to Israel or to the saints – I believe that it refers to the saints because Satan, the dragon, pursued her and her offspring who are *"those who keep God's commands and hold fast their testimony about Jesus."* (Revelation 12:17) The point I am making here is that God is capable of protecting the church and the saints even during the Tribulation where the church would be "out of the serpent's reach" in the wilderness (Revelation 12:14). The church that endures and follows God's commands faithfully may be kept from the Tribulation even while they are still on earth, just as how God protected Israel from the plagues in Egypt.

I believe that it would be apparent after reading John 17:15 together with Revelation 3:10 that Jesus' desire is not to remove the church from the world during the Tribulation but to keep them in it. God will protect the church just as He had protected the Israelites from the plagues of Egypt by making a distinction between them – the church may be spared God's wrath while still on earth, however, that does not mean that the church is exempt from persecution.

Jesus said to his disciples: *"In the world ye shall have tribulation: but be of good cheer; I have overcome the world."* (John

16:33) We should take heart that as Christians, even when we face overwhelming tribulation, we can overcome precisely because we have the overcomer with us. This should give us true comfort rather than to rely on thought of being raptured out of tribulation as our comfort. The real comfort we have is in Christ, the overcomer.

#4 The day of the Lord comes like a thief in the night and references to verses that Christ is coming "soon"

Pre-tribulationists point to Bible verses which emphasize the fact that Jesus is coming "soon" and the day of the Lord will come like a "thief" to justify that Christ is coming imminently and Christians will be caught by surprise when he comes "*at the hour when we do not expect him*". They claim that the New Testament speaks of the Lord's return as imminent and it could occur at any moment, and if the appearance of the Antichrist, the abomination that causes desolation and the unfolding events leading up to Christ's Second Coming must come first, then the command to watch for Christ's coming would be rendered meaningless. To the pre-tribulationist, the "imminency" of Christ's return is the central core teaching of the rapture before the Tribulation.

They point to several passages that emphasize the imminency of Christ's return: "*Therefore keep watch, because you do not know on what day your Lord will come.*" (Matthew 24:42) Jesus says: "*But about that day or hour no one knows, not even the angels in heaven, nor the Son, but only the Father. Be on guard!*

Be alert! You do not know when that time will come." (Mark 13:32) The Apostle Peter wrote: "*But the day of the Lord will come like a thief. The heavens will disappear with a roar.*" (2 Peter 3:10) The Apostle Paul also says: "*For you yourselves are fully aware that the day of the Lord will come like a thief in the night.*" (1 Thessalonians 5:2) And references to the Lord Jesus coming soon are found in Revelation 22:7, Revelation 22:12 and Revelation 22:20. Pre-tribulationists argue that since the Lord Jesus is coming "soon", this suggests that he may come at any moment and his coming is imminent.

It is interesting to note that this question of the imminency of Christ's return was considered by the Apostle Peter himself. Peter writes that during the last days, scoffers will come and say "*Where is this 'coming' he promised? Ever since our ancestors died, everything goes on as it has since the beginning of creation.*" (2 Peter 3:3-4) Peter's reply is very interesting. He says "*But do not forget this one thing, dear friends: **With the Lord a day is like a thousand years, and a thousand years are like a day.** The Lord is not slow in keeping his promise, as some understand slowness. Instead he is patient with you, not wanting anyone to perish, but everyone to come to repentance.*" (2 Peter 3:8-9) (*emphasis added*) In other words, Peter hints that when the Lord Jesus says he is coming "soon", he is coming soon relative to God's timing. And Peter says that in God's timing, a thousand years are like a day that has just gone by. Therefore, any reference to the soonest of God's coming should be understood in the context of God's timing rather than the human notion of "soon" – which could be anything from tomorrow to next week at the latest.

However, I do believe that there is another reason why the Lord Jesus says that he is coming soon. The simple reason is that Revelation was written to describe what would take place in the future – and there will come a point in time in the future where Christ's coming would indeed be soon. Future generations reading the Book of Revelation maybe 100 years down the road could be extremely close to the coming of the Lord Jesus when the signs of his coming are fulfilled – in this respect, the coming of the Lord Jesus can truly be said to be very soon for them in every sense of the word "soon". Since the Bible was written for future generations of Christians, there will come a point in time in the future where the Lord's coming would be very soon indeed.

As for the scripture verses dealing with the notion that we will not know the day and hour of his coming – this has already been dealt with the earlier chapters but it is useful repeating some points here for completeness. The mere fact that we do not know the day and hour (even Jesus himself does not know) does not *ipso facto* mean that Jesus is coming imminently. We may not know the exact day or hour when the volcano will erupt, but we will certainly be able to see the signs that the volcano is close to eruption. Similarly, Christians do not know the exact day and hour of Christ's Second Coming, but they will certainly be able to see the signs of his Second Coming and know when he is very near the door. The Apostle Paul reminds Christians that they are children of the day and not children of the night – watchful Christians will not be caught by surprise when the Lord Jesus comes because they will be keeping watch.

Pre-tribulationists may counter and say that to watch for the signs would render watching the Second Coming of Jesus' meaningless, because then Christians will have to abandon the hope of his imminent coming if the signs of his coming are not fulfilled yet. This is a valid concern, and one that the Apostle Paul addresses in 1 Thessalonians 5:10. Apparently, some members of the church in Thessalonica had already passed away and those who were left behind thought that if they died before Christ' coming, they would miss out on his Second Coming – therefore their expectation and hope of Christ's return during their lifetime would be in vain. Paul comforts them by saying: *"He died for us so that, whether we are awake or asleep, we may live together with him"*. Therefore, even if we hope in vain that Christ would return during our lifetime and we do pass away before He comes, Paul reminds us that whether we are dead or alive, we will live together with Christ. Therefore, Paul says, encourage each other with these words – death does not mean we will not see Christ when he comes!

Remember that immediately after the Olivet Discourse, Jesus tells his disciples three parables – the parable of the wicked servant, the parable of the ten virgins and the parable of the bags of gold where he says that the bridegroom or master was a **long time coming**. The true test of faithfulness, as the Lord Jesus suggests, is not what you would do if you thought Christ was coming tomorrow or at any moment. Rather, the true test is what you would do if you knew Christ was not coming back in your lifetime. Would you still be faithful and true, or would you become like the wicked and complacent servant?

I believe that the Lord Jesus told his disciples these parables precisely to drive home the point that he was not looking for those who serve him because they were in "panic" mode or thought that he was coming tomorrow or at any moment. Rather, the Lord Jesus was looking for the wise and faithful servant who continued to serve him faithfully even though he may not come back during the servant's lifetime. *"Who then is the wise and faithful servant?"* Jesus asks. We ought to think carefully what the Lord Jesus meant by these words.

Finally, I should mention that before the Lord Jesus was taken up to heaven, he told the Apostle Peter the kind of death that he would die. Jesus says: *"when you are old you will stretch out your hands, and someone else will dress you and lead you where you do not want to go."* (John 21:18-19) He said this precisely to indicate the kind of death that the Apostle Peter would die. And Jesus said to Peter: *"Follow me!"* Clearly, Peter knew that he was going to die before Christ returned to earth; he did not expect that the Lord Jesus was going to come and rapture him out of tribulation. The Lord Jesus also commanded his disciples to make disciples of all nations and preach the gospel to the whole world. His disciples knew that this would take a lot of time and would certainly not be fulfilled in their lifetimes. Therefore, the Apostles and the early church likely never held the view that Christ was coming imminently for the very reason that they knew that the gospel still had to be preached to all nations before Christ would come again.

I believe that the Lord Jesus gave the exhortation to be alert and to be on guard to guard against complacency and to deter Christians from becoming like the wicked servant who stopped watching for his master's coming. There will come a future generation of Christians in which Christ's coming can be said to be truly imminent when the signs of his coming have been fulfilled, and the exhortations to keep watch and be faithful are to guard against precisely the same kind of complacency that the wicked servant had in thinking that his master will not be coming in his lifetime. Jesus asks: *"when the Son of Man comes, shall he find faith on earth?"* (Luke 18:8) Will he find faithful servants on earth when he comes after a long time?

#5 There is no mention of any events that take place during the Second Coming in the rapture verses

Pre-tribulationists like to point out the contrasts between the rapture and the Lord's Second Coming to justify that they are two separate and distinct events. According to them, the translation of saints from their earthly bodies to glorified bodies occurs during the rapture. They point to 1 Corinthians 15:51-52 and 1 Thessalonians 4:15-17 as justification for this: *"in a flash... the dead will be raised imperishable, and we will be changed"*. Therefore, the rapture is an event in which Jesus comes for the church and all the saints on earth, while the Second Coming is characterized by the Lord coming with his saints to reign on earth (Zechariah 14:4-5). In other words, in the rapture, the Lord comes *for* his saints, while at his Second Coming, Christ comes *with* his saints.

They also point to what the Apostle Paul said in 1 Corinthians 15:51 that the rapture is a "mystery" which was not predicted by any Old Testament verse, while the Second Coming was clearly predicted in Old Testament scripture (Zechariah 14:4) Therefore, according to pre-tribulationists, this points to the rapture and Second Coming being separate distinguishable events.

John Walvoord, in his book *The Return of the Lord* (p. 88), points to several notable differences between the rapture and the Second Coming. First, during the rapture, the Lord Jesus comes for his saints and raptures the church *in the air* – the translation of believers into their glorified bodies occurs during this event. However, during the Second Coming, there is no translation or rapture at all; instead, the translated saints return back to earth to reign with Christ. Second, during the rapture the saints go back to heaven (they point to John 14:2 that Jesus goes to prepare a room for his disciples in his Father's house – or heaven – and returns to earth to take them there). By contrast, during the Second Coming, the Lord Jesus comes together with his saints back to earth to establish his kingdom. Third, the rapture is imminent and can occur at any moment, while the Second Coming follows definite predicted signs and occurs after the Tribulation. Fourth, the rapture only concerns believers before the Tribulation (i.e., church-age Christians), while the Second Coming affects all mankind. Fifth, there is no reference to Satan in the rapture, but there are references to the bounding of Satan and the judgment of the Antichrist and false prophet during the Second Coming. Sixth, the rapture marks the beginning of the Tribulation period where the church is snatched up to heaven, while the Second Coming marks the beginning of the Millennial Kingdom.

John Walvoord concludes that these contrasts should make it evident that the rapture or translation of the saints is quite a different event in character and form to the Second Coming. He argues that at the rapture, the Lord Jesus comes to take believers from earth to the Father's house (John 14:2), and at the Second Coming believers return from heaven back to earth. Since these contrasts are quite distinctive of each other, he argues that a pre-tribulation rapture position reconciles the differences between the rapture which is an imminent event and the Second Coming which occurs after the signs as described in Matthew 24 are fulfilled.

It is evident that pre-tribulationists face an immediate problem on how to interpret Matthew 24:31 at the end of the Tribulation where Jesus says: "*And he will send his angels with a loud trumpet call, and they will gather his elect from the four winds, from one end of the heavens to the other.*" Since pre-tribulationists argue that the rapture has already occurred, they must grapple with the question on what Matthew 24:31 was referring to. Some pre-tribulation scholars have attempted to reconcile Matthew 24:31 with the pre-tribulation view by saying that it does not refer to a rapture but rather a "gathering" of his elect to Jerusalem where he reigns. However, none of their arguments sound convincing to say the least. One can argue that the "gathering" of the saints is precisely what the Lord does in a rapture – to gather the saints to meet him in the air. Notice that in Paul's first letter to the Corinthians, he said that the rapture will occur "*in a flash, in the twinkling of an eye, **at the last trumpet**.*" (1 Corinthians 15:52) (*emphasis added*) The word '*last trumpet*' implies that it takes place at the very final trumpet call announcing the arrival of Christ. In Matthew 24, we see a similar reference to the trumpet "*he will send his angels with a loud trumpet call*". Notice that this trumpet call is also sounded simultaneously to announce the arrival of the Lord Jesus in Matthew 24:31. There is no mention whatsoever of two separate trumpet calls – one before the rapture and one announcing the Second Coming of Jesus Christ – in any of the synoptic gospels or the New Testament scripture. The clear meaning of scripture suggests that there will only be one trumpet call when Christ comes and he will rapture his saints to meet him in the air, which is exactly what the purpose of gathering his elect from the four winds is for. Nowhere in scripture does it say that Christ will be coming back twice in the future – the first time for his Bride and the second time to establish the Millennial Kingdom.

Pre-tribulationists mention quite a number of differences between the rapture and the Second Coming to support their view. I agree that there are certainly a number of differences between the rapture and the Second Coming in the sense that they are two distinct events. However, there is nothing to suggest that both the rapture and his Second Coming cannot occur simultaneously. Christ can logically come back to earth, rapture the saints to meet him in the air, and descend back to earth together with the saints to establish his kingdom with no difficulty. There is nothing in scripture to suggest that there must be intervening events between the rapture and his Second Coming. Paul says quite clearly that the rapture occurs at the "last trumpet" when Christ comes in 1 Corinthians 15:52. Therefore, there cannot logically be another trumpet call during the Second Coming, and Matthew 24:31 points to the fact that there will be a trumpet call when Christ comes. The easiest and most logical way to reconcile this is the post-tribulational view that the Second Coming and the rapture takes place simultaneously at the last trumpet call.

John Piper argues that the Greek word for "meet" used in the phrase *caught up to meet the Lord* in the air in 1 Thessalonians 4:17 is used two other times in the New Testament in Matthew

25:6 and Acts 28:15. In both instances, the word "meet" is always used in the context of meeting an important dignitary and accompanying them back to the place where you just went out from. Therefore, we see in Matthew 25:6 that the wise virgins went out to *meet* the bridegroom and then went back with him to the wedding banquet – and the door was shut (Matthew 25:10). In Acts 28:15 when Paul arrived at Rome, the brothers and sisters traveled as far as the Forum of Appius and the Three Taverns to *meet* Paul and accompany him back to Rome (Acts 28:15-16).

In this regard, John Piper argues that intention of the verse in 1 Thessalonians 4:17 is not a rapture in the sense that we rise to meet the Lord in the air and return to heaven for 7 years. Rather, it is a rapture in the sense that we meet the Lord in the air to welcome him back to earth, like how people will go out to greet a dignitary when he comes to a city or town, and accompany the dignitary back to his intended destination, which in the case of the rapture, is to Jerusalem. During the Second Coming, the Lord Jesus himself will stand on the Mount of Olives (Zechariah 14:4), the same place where he told his disciples about the signs of his coming in the Olivet Discourse in Matthew 24, in fulfilment of all that is to come.

The pre-tribulation view that the rapture and Second Coming are distinct events does not necessarily imply that they cannot occur simultaneously. A literal reading on 1 Corinthians 15:52 and Matthew 24 suggest that there will be one single glorious Second Coming of Jesus Christ. When he comes, the last trumpet will sound, Christians will be raptured to meet him in the air, and he then comes back with all the Christians to earth to establish the Millennial Kingdom.

Pre-tribulationists point to John 14:2 which states that the Lord Jesus is going to prepare a place for his disciples in his Father's house which logically infers that Christ is coming to take all his disciples to heaven. Therefore, they argue, during the rapture Christ will bring all saints to heaven which should be contrasted with the Second Coming where he comes back to earth to reign with his saints. Pre-tribulationists argue that since the "Father's house" in John 14:2 refers to heaven and not earth, Christians would be taken to heaven during the rapture and not earth. However, notice that immediately after the verse in John 14:2, Jesus said: *"And if I go and prepare a place for you, I will come again, and receive you unto myself; that **where I am, there ye may be also**."* (*emphasis added*) The whole point that the Lord Jesus was making here is that he is coming to take his disciples to where he is so that they may be with him. There is nothing here which implies that Christians must be taken up to heaven immediately after the rapture, or anything in these verses which tell us *when* Jesus would take us to the Father's house. The promise here is simply that Jesus will take us to the Father's house and that where he is, we will be also.

Pre-tribulationists may counter and say, *"Well, Jesus was clearly referring to his Father's house which refers to heaven, not earth. Therefore, the rapture must refer to taking Christians to heaven, not back to earth"*. However, even if the pre-tribulationists are right that we are raptured to heaven before the Tribulation, we would only be in heaven for 7 years – which is a rather short time to be in heaven compared to 1,000 years back on earth during the Millennial Kingdom. Is the ultimate fulfilment of John 14:2 to be in heaven for only 7 years? One has to wonder if being raptured to heaven for 7 years was really the true intention of the Lord Jesus in John 14:2.

It is very telling that a few verses later, Philip asks the Lord Jesus to *"show him the Father"* (John 14:8). The Lord Jesus said *"anyone who has seen me has seen the Father. How can you say, 'Show us the Father'? Don't you believe that I am in the Father, and that the Father is in me?"* (John 14:9-10) Lord Jesus then goes on to say that he and the Father are One, which suggests that where the Son is residing, there the Father is. In other words, where the Lord Jesus is, there the Father will be as well. Since the Lord Jesus would be on earth reigning together with Christians during the Millennial Kingdom, are pre-tribulationists prepared to tell Jesus that we are in fact not in the Father's house but on earth with him? The pre-tribulationist may ask the Lord Jesus to "show us the Father's house in heaven" and Jesus could very well reply "where I am, there the Father's house is".

However, there will come a time in the future when we will be truly in the Father's house. In the Book of Revelation, we see a "new heaven and a new earth" and the Holy City, the new Jerusalem, coming down out of heaven from God, prepared as a bride beautifully dressed for her husband (Revelation 21:2). The Lord Jesus promised us that those who are "victorious" will inherit all these (Revelation 21:7). The Lord Jesus promised to take faithful Christians to the Father's House – which is the New Jerusalem – where they will be truly reunited with God. This is the place where *"the throne of God and of the Lamb will be in the city, and his servants will serve him. They will see his face, and his name will be on their foreheads."* (Revelation 22:3-4). We will truly be in the Father's house when everything has been accomplished, where Jesus is. It is in this respect that John 14:2 will come to its ultimate fruition, not just for a brief 7-year period as pre-tribulationists would have it.

The Lord Jesus keeps his promises, but not in the human sense of *immediacy* that it will be fulfilled tomorrow or immediately after the rapture. There will come a time when all Christians will indeed be in the Father's house forever. The real point, however, that the Lord Jesus was driving at in John 14:2-3 is that if the Lord Jesus goes to prepare a place for us, he will come back to take us to be with him where he is. Paul says, *"And so we will be with the Lord forever."* (1 Thessalonians 4:17) We will one day truly be in the Father's house forever, and that is the ultimate comfort we have as Christians and the true fulfilment of John 14:2.

#6 A time interval is needed between the rapture and the Second Coming

Pre-tribulationists argue that a time interval is needed between the rapture of the church and the Second Coming for unsaved people to come to faith in Christ during the Tribulation (i.e., tribulation saints), so that these tribulation saints may enter the Millennial Kingdom in their earthly bodies. In his book *The Rapture Question*, John Walvoord writes that the scriptures are specific that during the Millennial, tribulation saints will *"build houses and bear children, and have normal, mortal lives on earth."* (Walvoord, p. 86) However, John argues that *"if all believers are translated and all unbelievers are put to death at the beginning of the Millennial Kingdom, there will be no one left to populate the earth and fulfill these Scriptures."* (Walvoord, p. 86) According to pre-tribulationists, it is necessary to address the question of who is going to populate the earth during the Millennial if all the saints are raptured at the end of the Tribulation at the Second Coming. They argue that this question is readily reconciled if one adopts the pre-tribulation view of the rapture.

Second, pre-tribulationists point to the fact that all believers must face the judgment seat of Christ (2 Corinthians 5:10) They argue that since the church is pictured in heaven as the bride that has made herself ready in fine linen (Revelation 19:7-8), therefore the church must be made ready during the 7 years in heaven to be presented as the Bride of Christ during the Second Coming. This would, according to pre-tribulationists, require a time interval which the pre-tribulation view explains well. It would be impossible for the church to be ready as the Bride of Christ if the judgment of the Gentiles took place after the Second Coming and was not separated by a time gap.

Third, pre-tribulationists point to a passage in Matthew 25 concerning the separation of sheep and goats when Jesus comes back to earth. In that passage, the Lord Jesus said that when the "*Son of Man comes in all his glory, and all the angels with him, he will sit on his glorious throne. All the nations will be gathered before him, and he will separate the people one from another as a shepherd separates the sheep from the goats.*" (Matthew 25:31-33). Jesus then goes on to say that those "sheep" who are the righteous ones will be invited to take their inheritance in the kingdom prepared for them since the creation of the world, while the "goats" will depart from him into the eternal fire prepared for the devil and his angels. John Walvoord points out that if "*the translation took place during the Second Coming, then there would be no need to separate the sheep from the goats at a subsequent judgment*" (Walvoord, p. 274) since the separation would have taken place itself during the rapture between believers and unbelievers. As such, the pre-tribulation view solves this issue through the 7-year gap where those tribulation saints are the "sheep" that are separated from the "goats" which refer to the rest of the unbelievers that come out of the Tribulation.

I will deal with each of these points in chronological order.

The survivors from all the nations that had attacked Jerusalem will populate the earth during the Millennial Kingdom

As to the first point raised by pre-tribulationists that if all believers are raptured at the end of the Tribulation and unbelievers are put to death at the beginning of the Millennial Kingdom (according to their interpretation of Matthew 25:31-43) and that there would be no one to populate the Millennial Kingdom, the scripture is clear on who exactly will be populating the Millennial Kingdom. The Book of Zechariah is crystal clear that when the Lord comes during the Second Coming and fights against the nations that attack Jerusalem, the survivors of those who attacked Jerusalem will populate the Millennial Kingdom:

> "*Then the **survivors from all the nations** that have attacked Jerusalem will go up year after year to worship the King, the Lord Almighty, and to celebrate the Festival of Tabernacles. If any of the peoples of the earth do not go up to Jerusalem to worship the King, the Lord Almighty, they will have no rain.*" (Zechariah 14:16-17) (*emphasis added*)

Therefore, since the rapture will take all believers out of the world at the Second Coming, those who are left behind – the survivors from the nations that have attacked Jerusalem – will be left to populate the Millennial Kingdom. Zechariah tells us that they will worship the Lord Jesus and go up to Jerusalem to celebrate the Festival of Tabernacles. The punishment for not going to Jerusalem to celebrate the Festival of the Tabernacles is also set out clearly in Zechariah 14:17 – those nations that do not go up will have no rain. During the Millennial Kingdom, there will be an extended period of peace on the earth and all the promises set out in Isaiah concerning the blessings during the Millennial Kingdom will be fulfilled. These survivors clearly do not refer to tribulation saints as these are the very people from the nations that the Lord goes out to fight against at the Second Coming (Zechariah 14:3).

Christ comes for his church first before the judgment seat of Christ. The judgment seat of Christ, or the Great White Throne judgement, serves two different purposes for Christians and unbelievers

The second point that 2 Corinthians 5:10 spells out that everyone will stand before the judgment seat of Christ and that the church, which is the Bride of the Lamb, must be made ready before the Second Coming – it should be noted that the Bible does not tell us in 2 Corinthians 5:10 when exactly Christians must stand before the judgment seat of Christ – it is silent on this point. It does not actually say that raptured believers will appear before the judgment seat of Christ during the Tribulation, assuming that they would be raptured before the Tribulation in the first place. The verse simply states that everyone must appear before the judgment seat of Christ, so that *"each of us may receive what is due us for the things done while in the body, whether good or bad."* (2 Corinthians 5:10) The Book of Revelation does describe the Great White Throne judgment where all the dead will be judged according to what they had done as recorded in the books. However, pre-tribulationists argue that the Great White Throne judgment is a judgment only for unbelievers and that believers will not be judged here. According to them, believers will be judged at the judgment seat of Christ which is a separate event that takes place in heaven during the 7 years of the Tribulation and is distinct from the Great White Throne judgment.

I believe that the judgment seat of Christ that the Apostle Paul wrote about in 2 Corinthians 5:10 is the Great White Throne judgment set out in Revelation 20:11, for the simple reason that during this judgment, references are made to the book of life: *"another book was opened, which is the book of life."* (Revelation 20:12) John writes that *"anyone whose name was not found written in the book of life was thrown into the lake of fire."* (Revelation 20:15) The logical implication of this verse is that anyone whose names was found written in the book of life would receive eternal life and enter the "new heaven and new earth" described in Revelation 21. If the Great White Throne judgment is purely reserved for unbelievers, why the need for the book of life if nobody's names would be written in it?

Pre-tribulationists argue that Revelation 19:7-8 suggests that the Bride of the Lamb has made herself ready and is dressed in fine linen, and therefore the Bride must first go through the judgment seat of Christ in heaven to get ready. This is mere speculation as nothing in these verses indicates that the Bride needs to stand before the judgment seat of Christ to be judged to get ready. These verses simply suggest that the Bride was covered in righteousness, as John clearly states: *"for the fine linen is the righteousness of saints."* (Revelation 19:8 KJV) Nothing in these verses state that the Bride appears before the judgment seat of Christ during the 7 years of Tribulation or is ready because she has been judged. Rather, the church is prepared as the Bride because of the righteousness of the saints.

There is no doubt that Christ comes for his Bride first at the rapture: *"And so we will be with the Lord forever."* (1 Thessalonians 4:17) The Bride is ready to be united with Christ because she is clothed in righteousness (Revelation 19:7-8) At the Second Coming, the Lord Jesus comes and raptures the church to meet him in the air, and the raptured saints accompany Jesus back to earth to establish and reign in the Millennial Kingdom. At the end of the Millennial Kingdom, Satan and all the peoples of the earth will be judged at the Great White Throne judgment (Matthew 25:34, Revelation 20:11). This judgment includes believers, but their names will be found in the book of life and they will enter into eternal life – conversely all those who are not found in the book of life will be consigned to the lake of fire (Revelation 20:15). This would be in fulfilment of 2 Corinthians 5:10, which concerns the judgment seat of Christ. It should be noted that the judgment seat of Christ serves two different purposes for Christians and unbelievers. For Christians, they will be judged and/or rewarded according to what they have done in the body. For unbelievers, they will be judged according to their works and if their names are not found in the book of life, will be cast into the lake of fire. Jesus will judge all of humanity with justice and in righteousness.

After the Great White Throne judgment, there is a "new heaven and new earth" where the righteous saints will inherit the kingdom prepared from the creation of the world (Matthew 25:34) It is there that John describes: "*I saw the Holy City, the new Jerusalem, coming down out of heaven from God, prepared as a bride beautifully dressed for her husband.*" (Revelation 21:2) Notice that the true Bride of the Lamb – the new Jerusalem – is only revealed after the Great White Throne judgment has concluded.

There should be no difficulty in reconciling the fact that Christians who put their faith and trust in Jesus Christ will be saved and raptured first to be with Christ, but will still have to face the judgment seat of Christ before they enter the new heaven and new earth, so that they may receive all that is due to them for their works – whether good or bad (2 Corinthians 5:10). This includes all the rewards that the Lord Jesus promised to those who are victorious and who serve him faithfully. The Book of Revelation only mentions one single Great White Throne judgment; there is not a single verse which mentions a separate judgment seat of Christ for the saints in heaven during the 7 years of Tribulation, assuming that the saints would be raptured before the Tribulation in the first place.

The separation of the sheep from the goats takes place during the Great White Throne judgment, when all nations and peoples are gathered before Christ

As to the third point that in Matthew 25:31-43 that Christ will gather all the nations and separate the sheep and goats, and the "sheep" who represent the righteous ones will inherit eternal life while the "goats" who represent those who reject Christ will be cast in the lake of fire – it should be noted that this passage does not actually tell us when this separation of "sheep" from the "goats" will occur. It simply tells us that when Jesus comes, he will sit on his glorious throne, and will gather the nations (or all peoples) before him to be judged. Notice that Matthew 25:41 mentions the wicked and the unbelievers as thrown into *"eternal fire prepared for the devil and his angels"* – however, Revelation 19:20 tells us that only the Antichrist and the false prophet will be thrown into the lake of fire at the Second Coming. Satan will be judged after the end of the Millennial Kingdom (Revelation 20:10), followed by the dead who will be judged at the Great White Throne judgment (Revelation 20:11). Those whose names are not written in the book of life will be thrown into the lake of fire.

Pre-tribulationists would have to ask the question whether Matthew 25:31-43 only concerns tribulation saints and unbelievers at the time of the Second Coming. According to their literal interpretation of Matthew 25:31-43, they claim that at the Second Coming, tribulation saints are the "sheep" or the righteous ones who enter the kingdom, while the "goats" or unbelievers will be thrown into the lake of fire. This probably explains why John Walvoord thought that all unbelievers will be put to death at the beginning of the Millennial Kingdom, based on his interpretation of Matthew 25:31-43. However, notice that in Zechariah 14:16-17, we are told that those who enter the Millennial Kingdom are the survivors of all nations who attacked Jerusalem and who will go up every year to worship the Lord. Clearly, the survivors of all those nations who attacked Jerusalem do not refer to believers – they are unbelievers that have not been raptured during the Second Coming and are from nations that God Himself fought against during the Second Coming. The pre-tribulation view that all unbelievers would have been killed in the lake of fire in Matthew 25:41 at the Second Coming does not accord with Zechariah 14:16-17 which states that the survivors of all those nations who attacked Jerusalem – the unbelievers – will go up every year to worship the Lord. Neither does it accord with Revelation 20:11-12 which states that all peoples will be judged at the Great White Throne judgment and those whose names are not found in the book of life will be thrown into the lake of fire, which takes place only after the Millennial Kingdom. These events clearly do not take place during the Second Coming but rather at the Great White Throne judgment.

Quite evidently, the language of Matthew 25:31-43 describes the judgment for all nations through the eons of time, including the righteous and the wicked among those who had died. Those who had died would need to receive resurrection bodies to stand trial before the throne of Christ. Those who are thrown into the lake of fire – the second death – are those people whose names are not written in the book of life (Revelation 20:14). We know that the judgment of the dead occurs only during the Great White Throne judgment, which occurs after the Millennial Kingdom. Therefore, Matthew 25:31 which describes Christ sitting on his glorious throne accords more accurately with Revelation 20:11 where Christ is described to sit on the Great White Throne as the righteous judge. This would be done in fulfilment of 2 Corinthians 5:10 that everyone – believers and unbelievers – must all appear before the judgment seat of Christ to receive what is due to them.

There is no evidence from a plain reading of 2 Corinthians 5:10 and Matthew 25:31-46 and Revelation 20:11-12 that there are three separate judgments – the first for the raptured church in heaven during the 7 years of Tribulation, the second for unbelievers who will be put to death at the Second Coming and the third for all unbelievers through the ages at the Great White Throne judgment – as pre-tribulationists claim. Instead, the Bible is clear that there will be one single Great White Throne judgment after the end of the Millennial Kingdom for everyone, where those whose names are not found in the book of life are thrown into the lake of fire (Revelation 20:15). The logical implication of this verse is that those whose names are found in the book of life will not be thrown into the lake of fire. After this, all those whose names are found in the book of life will see the "new heaven and new earth" where the Bride of Christ has been fully prepared and dressed beautifully for her husband. The only hope that Christians have at the Great White Throne judgment is for their names to be found in the book of life.

The contextual interpretation of these passages together with Zechariah 14:16 supports a post-tribulation rapture where the saints and elect will be raptured at the end of the Tribulation to be with the Lord. The Lord will wage war against the nations that attacked Jerusalem and the survivors of those nations who attacked Jerusalem will enter the Millennial Kingdom on earth. These survivors will go up to Jerusalem to worship the Lord every year. At the end of the Millennial Kingdom, the Lord Jesus will judge Satan and all the dead at the Great White Throne judgment, ushering in the new heaven and new earth where all the saints are pictured as the Bride of the Lamb beautifully dressed for her husband in the new Jerusalem. Christians will receive all the rewards due to them at this judgment. This would be in fulfilment of Matthew 25:31-43 where Jesus judges all peoples of the earth and separates the sheep from the goats, and where the righteous ones will receive eternal life and the kingdom prepared since the creation of the world as their inheritance (Matthew 25:31-43, Revelation 21:7).

#7 Post-tribulationism denies the imminent return of Christ

Pre-tribulationists point to the fact that the post-tribulation view rejects the very hope that Christ is coming imminently to rapture the church, and that it could happen at any moment. We have dealt with this point in the earlier chapter, but it is worth restating some of the points here for the sake of completeness, since this is a very common argument that is used against a post-tribulation rapture.

According to pre-tribulationists, the coming of the Lord Jesus is imminent because several scripture verses mention the imminency of Christ's return: exhortations to watch and wait for his coming as the blessed hope (1 Thessalonians 1:10, Titus 2:13, 1 Peter 1:13) and references to the day of the Lord "coming like a thief in the night" (1 Thessalonians 5:2, Mathew 24:43, 2 Peter 3:10), as well as scripture verses that point to the fact that we will not know the day and hour which the Lord will come (Matthew 24:44). Pre-tribulationists argue that if either the appearance of the Antichrist, the Abomination of Desolation and the persecution of Christians takes place first before Christ's coming, this would render the command to watch for Christ's coming meaningless. In this regard, only a pre-tribulation view that teaches an imminent rapture will truly account for the fact that we are to keep watch and not be caught by surprise when Jesus comes suddenly for the church or the body of Christ. I will deal with each of these arguments in consecutive order.

Exhortations in scripture to watch and wait for Jesus' coming

Pre-tribulationists point to the fact that Jesus himself told his disciples to keep watch: "*Therefore keep watch, because you do not know on what day your Lord will come*" (Matthew 24:42) and that the appearing of the Lord Jesus is our "*blessed hope*" (Titus 2:13). They argue that the command to keep watch would be rendered meaningless if Christians could see the signs of Jesus' coming, because then Christians would not be caught by surprise.

The point that the Lord Jesus was making in Matthew 24:42 however, was not that he would catch the faithful and wise servant by surprise, but rather he would catch the wicked and lazy servant by surprise. Notice that immediately after the Olivet Discourse, the Lord Jesus went on to tell his disciples three parables – the parable of the wicked servant, the parable of the ten virgins and the parable of the bags of gold where the single commonality is that the bridegroom or master was a "long time coming" (Matthew 24:48, Matthew 25:5, Matthew 25:19). The master only comes on a day and at an hour that a wicked servant would not expect him (Matthew 24:50), simply because the wicked and lazy servant is not watching or does not recognize the signs of his master's coming. Notice that the element of surprise here is only reserved for the wicked and lazy servant who does not keep watch. Clearly, these verses do not convey the impression that Christ would be returning imminently to his disciples; the exhortation was to be watchful so that when he comes, his disciples would be ready for him. What then are his disciples watching for? I believe that they are watching for the signs of his coming and preparing themselves for the big trouble because earlier on, they asked the Lord Jesus what would be the signs of his coming and of the end of the age (Matthew 24:3) and Jesus told them all the signs of his coming in Matthew 24.

The real test of faithfulness, as the Lord Jesus suggests in these parables, is not what you would do if you thought your master was coming tomorrow or at any moment. The real test is what you would do if your master was a long time coming, or if your master was not coming back in your lifetime. Would you stay faithful and true and continue serving him?

I believe that the Lord Jesus gave these parables precisely because he was looking for disciples that served him faithfully and not because they were in "panic" mode that he would be coming at any moment and scrambled to get things right with God. The wise and faithful servant is the one who perseveres in the faith even if he knows that his master is not coming for a long time or even in his lifetime. We have the example of the Apostle Peter, who knew the kind of death he would die because Jesus told him. Certainly, he was not expecting Jesus to come and rapture him. The early church also knew that they had to first preach the gospel to all nations before Christ comes again, which takes time.

References to the day of the Lord coming like a thief in the night

Pre-tribulationists point to passages of scripture that describe the day of the Lord coming like a "thief in the night" to emphasize the element of surprise (1 Thessalonians 5:2, Mathew 24:43, 2 Peter 3:10).

It should be noted however, that the Apostle Paul, after writing to the church in Thessalonica that the day of the Lord comes like a thief in the night, immediately goes on to tell the church: *"But you, brothers and sisters, are not in darkness so that this day should surprise you like a thief."* (1 Thessalonians 5:4) Paul then goes on to say that Christians are children of the **light**, which directly contrasts the day of the Lord coming like a thief in the **night**. Paul suggests that watchful Christians would not be caught off guard when the day of the Lord comes precisely because they are children of the light; the element of surprise is not reserved for Christians. They know what to watch for before Jesus comes back to earth. This is in contrast to the world which lives in darkness and does not recognize the signs of his coming.

Pre-tribulationists may counter and say that the imminency of Christ's return is what keeps Christians on their toes and prevents them from becoming complacent. In reality, this is a double-edged sword. We learn from Paul's second letter to the Thessalonians that the fear of Christ's imminent return was precisely what gripped the church in Thessalonica, when they received a report allegedly from Paul that the day of the Lord had come. Paul tells the church that the day of the Lord had not come because *"that day will not come until the rebellion occurs and the man of lawlessness is revealed.*" (2 Thessalonians 2:3) Clearly, Paul was telling the church in Thessalonica that they will see the man of lawlessness first before the day of the Lord. Paul then goes on to warn the Thessalonians about the deception that will take place when the lawless one comes (2 Thessalonians 2:9-10) and exhorts the church to "stand firm" and "hold fast" to the teachings passed on to them (2 Thessalonians 2:15).

The church in Thessalonica is a classic example of what happens when the church thinks that Christ is returning imminently or at any moment. People will start to quit their jobs and become idle – because if Christ is coming tomorrow or at any moment to rapture you to heaven, why bother to work? And Paul has to tell the church not to be idle and to guard against disruptive behavior. Clearly, Paul was guarding against this belief that Christ was coming imminently or at any moment and telling the church in Thessalonica not to be deceived.

It is interesting to note that although the Apostle Peter described that the day of the Lord will come like a thief (2 Peter 3:10), he also suggests that the "soonest" of the day of the Lord is not the kind of imminency that Christians expect to happen tomorrow or next week. He writes *"Do not forget…with the Lord a day is like a thousand years, and a thousand years are like a day."* (2 Peter 3:8) Instead, the Lord is patient, not wanting anyone to perish but to come to repentance (2 Peter 3:9). Therefore, references to the fact that the day of the Lord is coming "soon" (Revelation 22:7) and coming "like a thief in the night" should be understood in the context of God's timing. Peter clearly says that God is not slow in keeping his promises as human beings understand "slowness", but rather it is done in God's timing.

Abandoning the hope of Christ's imminent return

Finally, pre-tribulationists argue that to abandon the pre-tribulation view is to abandon the hope of Christ's imminent return. In other words, Christians are hoping in vain for Christ's return if his return is not imminent and intervening events have to take place before his coming. Logically, this would mean that some Christians who hope dearly that Christ would return during their lifetime would die even before they see Christ returning to earth.

In Paul's first letter to the Thessalonians, we clearly see him addressing this very concern in the church in Thessalonica had that those who had died had somehow missed the Second Coming or the resurrection. They were worried that they had hoped in vain for Christ to return and that those who had died would miss out on the resurrection. This is why the Apostle Paul wrote that they should not be uninformed about those who sleep in death (1 Thessalonians 4:13) and that the dead in Christ would rise first to meet the Lord in the air. Paul then goes on to say that whether we are awake or asleep, Christ died for us so that we may live together with him (1 Thessalonians 5:10). Therefore, Paul says, encourage each other with these words. The dead in Christ certainly did not hope in vain – because they will get the front row seat when Jesus comes at the rapture.

The simple and appropriate response to the pre-tribulationist who says that to abandon the pre-tribulation rapture is to abandon the hope of Christ's imminent return during our lifetime, is simply to say that whether we are alive or asleep, Christ died for us so that we may live together with him. Christians who have fallen asleep before the Second Coming will not miss out on the rapture and will rise to meet the Lord in the air when he comes. Therefore, we should encourage each other with these words.

Chapter 5

How Should Christians Prepare for the Tribulation?

If the rapture is not the next event on the prophetic calendar, it logically follows that the Tribulation is the very next event that Christians will go through in the future. None of this debate would make any practical sense unless it involved a discussion on how Christians should prepare for the Tribulation ahead of time. After all, the Lord Jesus warned us not to be deceived and to be prepared: *"See, I have told you ahead of time."* (Matthew 24:25)

Corrie ten Boom, the missionary who went through the holocaust and had been through jail and persecution herself for Jesus' sake, wrote in her 1974 letter from China to America's pastors concerning the rapture that there are three things Christians need to do to prepare for the coming Tribulation.

First, Christians need to know the Word of God by heart. Corrie writes: *"we need to feed on the word of God, digest it, make it part of our being*". The Word of God provides comfort and strength for God's people, and the Book of Revelation constantly reminds the church to be strong in persecution and to be victorious. The Lord Jesus said: "*in this world ye shall have tribulation*", however, Christians should cheer up because Christ has overcome the world. We can overcome because Christ has overcome and we have the overcomer with us.

Corrie wrote about her time in the Nazi concentration camps when she had no access to any Bible, so she stored up the Word of God in her heart. This was how she overcame tribulation by memorizing verses that helped her through tribulation, and through her paralysis that struck her later in life.

Second, Corrie writes that we need to develop a relationship with Jesus Christ. In other words, we need to develop a relationship with the living Christ who was raised from the dead and is sitting on the right hand of God.

Third, Corrie wrote that we need to be filled with the Holy Spirit in order to go through tribulation. "*This is absolutely necessary*", she writes, as those disciples could never have stood up to persecution in Jerusalem and in Rome if they had not received the Holy Spirit. Corrie wrote that each Christian needs to have their own Pentecost to receive the Holy Spirit – this is key for Christians to stand during the Tribulation – not by their own strength but by the power of God.

The Lord Jesus himself also spoke to his disciples on how to prepare for the Tribulation in the Olivet Discourse. Importantly, he told his disciples repeatedly not to be deceived: "*Watch out that no one deceives you*" (Matthew 24:4). Jesus warned against false messiahs and false prophets that would do signs and wonders to deceive, if it were possible, even the elect (Matthew 24:24). The only implication of such a warning given before and during the Tribulation is that Jesus has not come yet; only false messiahs will appear. In the Gospel of Luke, Jesus is recorded as saying that many will claim, *the time is near – do not follow them*" (Luke 21:8), which suggests that we should guard against any teaching that Christ is coming imminently or at any moment. Jesus tells us plainly that we should not follow them.

The Apostle Paul also warned the church in Thessalonica not to be deceived. He says, *"Don't let anyone deceive you"* (2 Thessalonians 2:3). The man of lawlessness will use all sorts of displays of power through signs and wonders to deceive the nations and serve the lie (2 Thessalonians 2:9-10). Paul tells the church to stand firm and hold fast to the teaching of the gospel, and to wait for the Lord Jesus from heaven. We need to watch that we are not deceived about the timing of the Lord's coming, and not be deceived by false messiahs and false prophets.

The Apostle Peter wrote that Christians should not be surprised at the fiery ordeal that has come to test them, but rather rejoice in the sufferings of Christ so that they may be overjoyed when Christ comes (1 Peter 4:12-13). Peter clearly knew that he was not going to be raptured before Christ came because the Lord Jesus told him the kind of death he would die. Jesus told Peter to follow him all the way – and Peter was indeed crucified in AD 64 when he was ordered to be executed by the Roman Emperor Nero.

I love the honesty of Jesus when he tells all Christians that in this world you will have tribulation. All three synoptic gospels tell Christians to take up the cross and follow Jesus, which is clearly not a pleasant and enjoyable thing to do. The cross is heavy and burdensome. When you read some of the troubles that the Apostle Paul went through – shipwrecks, jail time, flogging – it is certainly not a picture of comfort. Stephen, the first martyr, was stoned to death for his faith in Christ. The Book of Hebrews talks about Christians being thrown into prison, against the background of Christian suffering. It is certainly not an easy road for Christians when they encounter tribulation.

When we read the Book of Revelation, it becomes apparent that it is in fact a manual for martyrdom. Christians who are experiencing persecution in the local church understand the Book of Revelation precisely because it is addressed to Christians who are suffering. It is a comforting book for Christians experiencing persecution because Jesus promises that he will reward those who are victorious and who overcome. The whole purpose of the Revelation is to encourage Christians through persecution; it is not given to satisfy the reader's curiosity of what might take place in the future.

The reason why the pre-tribulation rapture view is precarious is because it gives Christians false hope that they will be taken out of the big trouble before it comes. It renders large parts of the Book of Revelation from Chapters 4-18 purely academic for Christians and claims that it only concerns tribulation saints in a different dispensation. The pre-tribulation view denies that the church has anything to do with Israel's ultimate salvation in the end times, which is fundamentally unbiblical and contrary to the Apostle Paul's teaching in Romans 11. It teaches that Christ is coming imminently, which is precisely what the Lord Jesus warned against when he said that many false teachers will claim that *"The time is near"* (Luke 21:8). The imminency of Christ's return is what the Apostle Paul warned against in his second letter to the Thessalonians, when the church started to become idle in expectation of Christ's imminent return due to a false report they had received. The pre-tribulation view does not accord with the Lord Jesus' own character when he prayed: *"I pray not that thou shouldest take them out of the world, but that thou shouldest keep them from the evil."* (John 17:15) The pre-tribulation view that Christians will be taken out of the world before tribulation comes is similar to the teaching of false prophets in the Book of Jeremiah when they say *"Peace, peace"* when there is no peace at all (Jeremiah 6:14). It is the message of comfort that the world likes to hear.

The Lord Jesus taught us to persevere through suffering: *"but the one who stands firm to the end will be saved."* (Matthew 24:13) Let us get ready for the big trouble, as the Apostle Paul wrote, by putting on faith and love as a breastplate, and the hope of salvation as a helmet so that we can stand firm to the very end when the Tribulation comes.

Chapter 6

Conclusion

What then should Christians say in response to these things? Paul asks: *"Shall tribulation, or distress, or persecution or famine, or nakedness, or peril, or sword separate us from the love of Christ?"* (Romans 8:35 KJV) Paul then goes on to say: *"As it is written, For thy sake we are killed all the day long; we are accounted as sheep for slaughter."* (Romans 8:36 KJV, Psalm 44:22 KJV). No, Paul says, in all these things we are more than conquerors through Christ who loved us.

The Lord Jesus died for us so that we may receive salvation by putting our faith and trust in him. He did not die to save Christians from 7 years of Tribulation, but rather from the eternal wrath of God – expressed in the lake of fire – where he will throw Satan and all who reject Christ at the great judgments set out in the Book of Revelation. He died so that the church may one day be united with Christ in heaven as the Bride of the Lamb.

The pre-tribulation rapture view is fundamentally unbiblical because it is contrary to the teachings of the Lord Jesus to persevere, to endure and to stand firm to the very end through the Tribulation. He warned us against rampant deception that will take place during the last days concerning his Second Coming and false teachers who say that the end is near and Christ is coming imminently. Jesus told us these things ahead of time precisely to prepare us for the Tribulation ahead of time. If we were to accept the pre-tribulation rapture view, then major parts of the Book of Revelation immediately cease to have any practical significance for Christians. It becomes a purely academic book. But the Bible was never meant to be a purely academic book to be studied without any practical implications. Paul says, *"all Scripture is God-breathed and is useful for teaching, rebuking, correcting and training in righteousness."* (2 Timothy 3:16-17) What then, is the practical significance of Revelation 4-18 for pre-tribulationists?

Much of the historical roots of the pre-tribulation dispensational view can be traced back to John Nelson Darby, who thought that since Christians are already united with the body of Christ, they would have nothing to wait for but Christ. He saw a change in dispensation during the Tribulation where God comes first to rapture the church out of the world and then deal with the Jewish remnant of Israel and unbelievers. Darby assumed that since the body of Christ had nothing to wait for but Christ, and God still had to settle the promises he made to Israel during the last days, he reasoned that the Lord would rapture the church out of the world first before he dealt with the nation of Israel.

Darby could not have been further from the truth by teaching that Matthew 24 taught *"Kingdom-truths"* and not *"Church-truths"*. He failed to see that the church, or the body of Christ, plays an essential role in the salvation of Israel at the last days. In this regard, the Apostle Paul writes that when the full number of Gentile believers have come in, then *"in this way all Israel will be saved"* (Romans 11:26) and *"the deliverer will come from Zion; he will turn godlessness away from Jacob."* (Isaiah 59:20) Both the church and Israel's salvation has always been inextricably tied together and dispensationalists fail to see that the church – the body of Christ – has a role in the ultimate salvation of Israel in the end times. It is therefore not surprising that many in the Brethren movement including George Muller and B. W. Newton parted ways with Darby on this view.

There is not a single Bible verse in the Old Testament or New Testament which states unequivocally that Jesus is coming two times in the future. The pre-tribulation rapture view is based on a series of logical deductions from scripture starting from John Nelson Darby that the church and Israel are two distinct and separate entities, and therefore God deals with the church and Israel in separate dispensations. But nothing could be further from the truth. When reading the words of the Lord Jesus in the synoptic gospels and in the Book of Revelation, it becomes apparent that the church and Israel are to go through the Tribulation together. The dispensational view that the church is not involved at all with the ultimate redemption of Israel during the Tribulation is not in line with scripture. While the Lord will surely keep the promises he made to Israel during the end times, the church has a role to play in bringing Israel to salvation when the full number of believers has come in: *"in this way all of Israel will be saved."* (Romans 11:26) Paul tells us that in Christ there is neither Jew nor Gentile, neither slave or free, for all are one in the Jesus Christ. Therefore, he says, *"if you belong to Christ, then you are Abraham's seed, and heirs according to the promise."* (Galatians 3:29) If the church and Israel are heirs according to the promise given to Abraham, it follows that the church will play a role in Israel's ultimate redemption so that both the Gentile church and Israel may be one in Christ: *"the deliverer will come from Zion; he will turn godlessness away from Jacob."* (Romans 11:26, Isaiah 59:20) During the last days of the Tribulation, Israel will look on Jesus, the one that they have pierced, and mourn for him as one mourns for an only child, and grieve bitterly for him as one grieves a firstborn son (Zechariah 12:10). All Israel will be saved in fulfilment of the Old Testament prophecies and be brought in oneness with the church in the Lord Jesus. And then the Lord Jesus comes back to reign on earth and raptures all believers, Gentile and Jewish, when the Bride has made herself ready at his Second Coming.

The teaching that the Lord Jesus is coming imminently is fundamentally unbiblical. It was the very same teaching that gripped the church in Thessalonica and caused some members to become idle and disruptive, and Paul had to write to them not to be idle and get back to work. When people start to take false presumptions about the Second Coming seriously, the consequence is that people may think, "Well, if Christ is coming tomorrow, why should I work?" and start to become idle. While pre-tribulationists may argue that to reject the teaching that Christ is coming imminently would make Christians complacent, the truth is that this teaching makes Christians equally complacent about the Tribulation. We should preach the gospel that Christ preached, not a gospel that relies on human logic and reason and deduction as the truth.

The true test of faithfulness, as the Lord Jesus suggests, is not what you would do if you thought Christ is coming tomorrow or at any moment. The true test of faithfulness is whether you would continue to be faithful even if you knew Christ was a long time coming or even not coming back in your lifetime. Would you remain faithful and true to the Word of God, just as the wise and faithful servant was? The Lord Jesus is not looking for disciples who serve him because they are in "panic" mode that he will come tomorrow, but rather for disciples who obey the command to serve him faithfully in righteousness.

Does this mean that even if Christ does not come in our lifetime, we would therefore hope in vain? Certainly not. The Apostle Paul tells us plainly that Christ died for us so that whether we are awake or asleep, we would live together with Christ. Therefore, we should encourage each other with these words. Death is not the end – those who are asleep in Christ will not miss the Second Coming but rise to meet him in the air when he comes. Salvation in the Lord Jesus is the real comfort that every Christian has – not the comfort of escaping the 7 years of Tribulation which will come on the earth in the future.

Before the Lord Jesus left his disciples, he told his disciples that they will face tribulation but encouraged them to be of good cheer because he had overcome the world: *"These things I have spoken unto you, that in me ye might have peace. In the world ye shall have tribulation: but be of good cheer; I have overcome the world."* (John 16:33 KJV) He prayed that Christians would not be taken out of the world but be protected from the evil one: *"My prayer is not that you take them out of the world but that you protect them from the evil one."* (John 17:15) He prayed that all believers – whether Jew or Gentile – would become one just as how he and the Father were one (John 17:20-21). How would the church and Israel become one in Christ if the church was raptured before all of Israel was brought to salvation? What did Jesus mean when he said in this world you will have tribulation, but we should be at peace and of good cheer? What did Jesus mean when he prayed that Christians should not be taken out of the world but rather to be kept from the evil one?

The simple truth from reading the Bible is that all Christians are to go through the Tribulation in the future: "He that endures to the end will be saved". Jesus promised us big trouble. Christians are going to suffer for his name's sake. Many will die and suffer terrible persecution. "But cheer up!", the Lord Jesus says, "I have overcome the world, so you can." "Peace I leave with you, my peace I give unto you, not as the world giveth. Let not your hearts be troubled, neither let it be afraid." The real comfort and peace that we have in the Lord Jesus is not the promise to escape from the Tribulation but rather, we can overcome tribulation precisely because we have the overcomer with us.

Before Jesus was crucified, he prayed: *"I pray also for those who will believe in me through their message, that all of them may be one, Father, just as you are in me and I am in you."* (John 17:20-21) At the very end, God will answer the Lord Jesus' prayer when both Israel and the church finally become one in Christ and have made themselves ready as his Bride at his Second Coming. "And so we will be with the Lord forever".

Let us get ready for trouble.

Bibliography

John F. Walvoord, *The Rapture Question: Revised and Enlarged Edition* (Grand Rapids: Zondervan, 1979)

John F. Walvoord, *The Return of the Lord* (Dunham Publishing Company, 1955)

R. A. Huebner, *John Nelson Darby: Precious Truths Revived and Defended, Volume One* (Present Truth Publishers, 2004)

Hal Lindsey, *The Late Great Planet Earth* (Zondervan, 1970)

Michael Williams, *This World is not My Home, The Origins and Development of Dispensationalism* (Mentor, 2003)

David Pawson, *Israel, the Church in the End Times* (Recorded at the International House of Prayer, Kansas City, 2002)

David Pawson, *The End Times (Matthew 24-25)* (Recorded at Changi Cove, Singapore, 2013)

John Phillips, *Exploring 1 & 2 Thessalonians (John Phillips Commentary Series)* (Kregel Academic & Professional, 2005)

John R. W. Stott, *The Gospel & the End of Time: The Message of 1 & 2 Thessalonians,* (Intervarsity Press 1991)

Arnold G. Fruchtenbaum, *The Footsteps of the Messiah: A Study of the Sequence of Prophetic Events* (Ariel Mininstries; First Edition, 1983)

Ruth B. Graham, *Letter to Dave MacPherson* (Little Piney Cove, Montreal, North Carolina, March 31, 1975)

John Piper, *What is the Rapture?* (Recorded at the Desiring God Foundation, December 21, 2018)

Thomas D. Ice, *Why I Believe the Bible Teaches Rapture Before Tribulation* (Liberty University, Article Archives, 2009)

Jonas E. Alexis, *Christianity and Rabbinic Judaism: A History of Conflict between Christianity and Rabbinic Judaism* (WestBow Press, 2013)

Charles Haddon Spurgeon, *The Sword and the Trowel: A Record of Combat With Sin and of Labour for the Lord* (Forgotton Books, 2018)

Ray Crocker, *The End Times Series* (Recorded at Heritage Baptist Church Singapore, 2022)